ON THE TRAGIC

MERIDIAN

Crossing Aesthetics

Werner Hamacher
& David E. Wellbery
Editors

Translated by
Paul Fleming

Stanford
University
Press

Stanford
California
2002

AN ESSAY ON THE TRAGIC

Peter Szondi

An Essay on the Tragic was originally published in German in 1961 under the title *Versuch über das Tragische* by Insel Verlag; it was republished in 1978 in Peter Szondi, *Schriften I*, © 1978, Suhrkamp Verlag, Frankfurt am Main.

Stanford University Press
Stanford, California

Printed in the United States of America
on acid-free, archival-quality paper

Library of Congress Cataloging-in-Publication Data

Szondi, Peter.
[Versuch über das Tragische. English]
An essay on the tragic / Peter Szondi; translated by Paul Fleming.
p. cm.
ISBN 0-8047-4237-5 (alk. paper)—ISBN 0-8047-4395-9 (pbk.: alk. paper)
1. Tragic, The. 2. Tragedy—History and criticism. I. Title.
BH301.T7 S9513 2002
809'.9162—dc21 2002002459

Original printing 2002

Last figure below indicates year of this printing:
11 10 09 08 07 06 05 04 03 02

Typeset by Alan Noyes
in 10.9/13 Adobe Garamond and Lithos Display

Contents

PART II. ANALYSES OF THE TRAGIC

If you do evil to us, it comes to us from ourselves.

—Agrippa D'Aubigné

When I think that I am satisfied and at ease,
I harm myself.

—Jean de Sponde

Introduction

Since Aristotle, there has been a poetics of tragedy. Only since Schelling has there been a philosophy of the tragic.[1] Composed as an instruction in writing drama, Aristotle's text strives to determine the elements of tragic art; its object is tragedy, not the idea of tragedy. Even when it goes beyond the concrete work of art and inquires into the origin and effect of tragedy, the *Poetics* remains empirical in its theory of the soul. The realizations it thereby achieves (the imitative instinct as art's origin and catharsis as tragedy's effect) are meaningful not in themselves, but rather in their significance for tragic poetry, whose laws are to be derived from them. Modern poetics is essentially based upon the work of Aristotle; the history of modern poetics is the history of his reception and influence. This history can be understood as adoption, expansion, and systemization, as well as misunderstanding and critique. Aristotle's prescriptions regarding closure and the plot's scope played a particularly important role in classicism's theory of the unity of time, space, and action and its correction by Lessing. The same applies for his theory of fear and pity, whose numerous and contradictory interpretations yield a historical poetics of tragedy.[2]

The philosophy of the tragic rises like an island above Aristotle's powerful and monumental sphere of influence, one that knows neither national nor epochal borders. Begun by Schelling in a thoroughly non-programmatic fashion, the philosophy of the tragic runs though the Idealist and post-Idealist periods, always assuming a new form. If one counts Kierkegaard among the German philosophers and leaves aside his students such as Unamuno,[3] the philosophy of the tragic is proper to German philosophy. Until this day, the concept of the tragic[4] has remained fundamentally a German one. Nothing is more characteristic of this fact than a parenthetical remark with which Marcel Proust begins a letter: "You will see the entire tragedy, as the German critic Curtius would say, of my situation."[5] Therefore, the first part of the following study, dealing with definitions of the tragic, contains only the names of German philosophers and poets, while the second part considers the works of Greek antiquity, the Spanish, English, and German Baroque, as well as French and German classicism and its dissolution.

Just as one cannot reproach Aristotle's *Poetics* for lacking insight into the phenomenon of the tragic, one cannot deny from the outset the validity of the theory of the tragic produced by German philosophy after 1800 for earlier tragic poetry. To understand the historical relation prevailing between nineteenth-century theory and seventeenth-century and eighteenth-century practice, one must assume that the flight of Minerva's owl over this landscape also begins only with the onset of dusk.[6] And yet, only the commentaries constituting the book's first section can determine to what extent the definitions of the tragic in Schelling and Hegel, in Schopenhauer and Nietzsche, take the place of tragic poetry (whose time seems to have come when these authors were writing) and to what extent these definitions describe tragedies or even their models.

The first section simply contains commentaries, not exhaustive presentations, let alone criticism. The commentaries refer to texts assembled, apparently for the first time here, from the philosophical and aesthetic writings of twelve thinkers and poets between 1795 and 1915. These commentaries can neither critically penetrate the systems from which the definitions of the tragic are extracted nor do justice to their singularity. Rather, the commentaries must, with few exceptions, make do with inquiring into the status of the tragic in the relevant thought structure and, thereby, partially compensate for the injustice done to it by tearing out quotes. Furthermore, the task of the commentaries is to make the various definitions of the tragic comprehensible by revealing a more or less concealed structural element that is common to all. This structural moment obtains its significance when one reads the various thinkers' definitions not in view of their specific philosophies, but rather in view of the possibility of analyzing tragedies with their help, that is, in the hope of securing a general concept of the tragic. The exceptions, though, are those commentaries that have to wrest the meaning from a difficult text (such as Hölderlin's fragment) or that dig beneath a definition of the tragic and look for its origin at a point where the tragic is apparently not yet addressed, but where the explanation for its later definition is found. This is the case in the Hegel commentary, which constitutes the basis for the other interpretations, just as Hegel must be named before all others at the beginning of this book, for its insights are indebted to Hegel and his school, without which it never could have been written.

PART I

The Philosophy of the Tragic

§ 1 Schelling

> It has often been asked how Greek reason could bear the contradictions of Greek tragedy. A mortal, destined by fate to become a criminal, fights *against* this fate, and yet he is horribly punished for the crime, which was the work of fate! The *reason* for this contradiction, what made it bearable, lay deeper than the level at which it has been sought: It lay in the conflict of human freedom with the power of the objective world. In this conflict, the mortal necessarily had to succumb if the power was a superior power—a *fatum*. And yet, since he did not succumb *without a fight*, he had to be *punished* for this very defeat. The fact that the criminal, who only succumbed to the superior power of fate, was *punished* all the same—this was the recognition of human freedom, an *honor* owed to freedom. It was by *allowing* its hero to *fight* against the superior power of fate that Greek tragedy honored human freedom. In order not to exceed the limits of art, Greek tragedy was obliged to have the hero *succumb*; but in order to compensate for this humiliation of human freedom imposed by art, it also had to allow him to *atone* and *make amends*—even for a crime committed through *fate*. . . . It was a *great* thought: To willingly endure punishment even for an *unavoidable* crime, so as to prove one's freedom precisely through the loss of this freedom and perish with a declaration of free will.[1]

By no longer focusing on the effect that the tragic has on the audience but on the phenomenon of the tragic itself, this interpretation of *Oedipus Rex* and of Greek tragedy in general commences the history of the theory of the tragic. The text comes from the last of the *Philosophical Letters on Dogmatism and Criticism*, which Schelling wrote in 1795 at the age of twenty. In these letters, Schelling contrasts the teachings of Spinoza and

Kant (which Fichte already had called the only two "completely consistent systems")[2] and at the same time attempts to guard critical philosophy against lapsing into its own dogmatism. In a letter to Hegel from this period, Schelling writes: "The real difference between critical and dogmatic philosophy appears to be that the former proceeds from the absolute I (which has yet to be conditioned by an object), while the latter proceeds from the absolute object or non-I."[3] This sentence corresponds to the conflicting meanings that the two theories attribute to freedom, which for Schelling constitutes "the essence of the I," the "alpha and the omega of all philosophy."[4] In dogmatism, the subject chooses the absolute as the object of its knowledge and therefore pays the price of "absolute passivity." Criticism, on the contrary, which posits everything in the subject and thus negates everything in the object, "is a striving for immutable selfhood, unconditional freedom, and unbounded activity."[5] Schelling himself, it seems, understood that both of these possibilities disregard the power of the objective, for even when the objective is victorious thanks to the absolute passivity of the subject, it owes its victory to the subject itself. Schelling therefore has the fictive addressee of his letters indicate a third possibility, one that is no longer derived from the presuppositions of philosophical systems, but from life and its presentation in art. "You are right," the tenth letter begins, "one thing still remains—to *know* that there is an objective power which threatens to destroy our freedom and, with this firm and certain conviction in our hearts, to fight *against* it, to summon up all our freedom and to thus perish."[6] And yet, as though shrinking from the recognition of the objective, the young Schelling permits this struggle only in tragic art, not in life. This struggle, Schelling writes, "could not become a system of action for the simple reason that such a system presupposes a race of Titans, in the absence of which, however, it would undoubtedly have the most ruinous consequences for humanity."[7] Schelling thus subscribes to the idealistic faith that believes it has the tragic under its power and that acknowledges it only because it has discovered a meaning in it: the assertion of freedom. Accordingly, he sees the tragic process in *Oedipus Rex* as significant not in itself, but only in view of its telos. Nonetheless, the structure of the tragic particular to this process is evident. In Schelling's interpretation, the tragic hero does not merely succumb to the superior power of the objective, but is also additionally punished for succumbing, for taking up the struggle at all. Hence, the positive value of his attitude—the will to freedom, which is "the essence of his I"—turns against him. Following Hegel, this process can be called dialectical.[8] Admittedly, Schelling had in mind the assertion of freedom that is paid for with the hero's demise, for the possibility of a purely tragic process was alien to him. Yet one sentence grounds all of Schelling's philosophical endeavors concerning the problem of the tragic: It was a great thought "to willingly endure punishment even for an *unavoidable* crime, so as to prove one's freedom precisely through the loss of this freedom." Within this sentence one can already hear the somber theme that later can no longer be drowned out by any consciousness of the triumph of the sublime: the knowledge that something great and lofty was destroyed precisely by what should have saved it.

> The essence of *tragedy* is . . . a real conflict between freedom in the subject and objective necessity. This conflict does not end with the defeat of one or the other, but rather with both of them simultaneously appearing as conquerors and conquered in perfect indifference.[9]

> The conflict of freedom and necessity truly [exists] only where the latter undermines the will itself, and where freedom is fought on its own ground.[10]

Schelling's interpretation of tragedy in the *Lectures on the Philosophy of Art*, first delivered in 1802–3, explicitly refers to his earlier book on dogmatism and criticism. The starting point, however, is no longer a third possible relation between subject and object that is reserved especially for art and exists alongside the other two fundamentally possible relations. Rather, the starting point is developed from Schelling's philosophy of identity and assumes a central position in his aesthetics founded upon this philosophy. While Schelling posits God as the "infinite ideality grasping all reality within itself,"[11] he defines the beautiful as the "forming-into-one [*Ineinsbildung*] of the real and the ideal," as "the indifference of freedom and necessity, viewed in a real entity."[12] The three poetic genres appear as different manifestations of this identity. In the epic, Schelling sees

> a state of innocence, so to speak, where everything that will later only exist in dispersion or that will only return to a state of unity after a period of dispersion is still together and one. In the progress of culture [*Bildung*], this identity flared up into conflict in the lyrical poem. It was only with the

> ripest fruit of later culture that unity itself was reconciled with conflict on a higher level and that the two became one again in a more perfect formation [*Bildung*]. This higher identity is drama.[13]

Thus, Schelling's entire system, whose essence is the identity of freedom and necessity, culminates in his definition of the tragic process as the restoration of this indifference in conflict. The tragic is once again understood as a dialectical phenomenon, for the indifference of freedom and necessity is possible only at the price of the conqueror simultaneously being the conquered, and vice versa. The site of the conflict is not an intermediate zone that remains external to the struggling subject; rather, it has been transferred into freedom itself, which, now at odds with itself, becomes its own adversary.

§ 2 Hölderlin

> The significance of tragedies can be understood most easily by way of paradox. Since all potential is divided justly and equally, everything that is original appears not in its original strength, but rather, properly, in its weakness. Hence, appearance and the light of life quite properly belong to the weakness of every whole. Now in the tragic, the sign in itself is insignificant, without effect, but the original is openly revealed. Properly speaking, the original can appear only in its weakness; but insofar as the sign in itself is posited as insignificant = 0, the original, the hidden ground of every nature, can also present itself. If nature properly presents itself in its weakest talent, then, when it shows itself in its strongest talent, the sign = 0.[1]

Written between 1798 and 1800,[2] this fragment, along with the two other Homburg texts on the tragic ("The Ground for Empedocles" and the essay "Becoming in Passing Away"), takes as its starting point the concept of nature. Like the other two texts, its intention is to grant man a position vis-à-vis nature that simultaneously shows man as nature's servant and nature as dependent on man. In a letter to his brother of June 4, 1799, Hölderlin speaks of the "paradox, . . . that the instinct for art and cultivation, with all of its modifications and varieties, is a proper service that men perform for nature."[3] The fragment quoted above uses this paradox to explain the meaning of tragedy. One finds its fundamental idea once again in a letter to Sinclair of December 24, 1798, where Hölderlin describes the fact "that no power in heaven and on earth is monarchical" as "the first condition of all life and all organization."[4] Because "all potential is divided justly and equally," what is original in its essence, nature, cannot simultaneously "appear in its original strength, but rather, properly, only in its weakness." "Properly" here means: in accordance with its own possibility, from its own power. This dialectic, whereby the strong can appear only as weakness and needs something weak so that its strength can appear, grounds the necessity of art. In art, nature no longer appears "properly," but through the mediation of a sign. In tragedy, this sign is the tragic hero. Insofar as he can do nothing against the power of nature and is destroyed by it, he is "insignificant" and "without effect." But in the tragic hero's demise, when the sign = 0, nature presents itself as a conqueror "in its strongest talent," and "the original is openly revealed." Hölderlin thus interprets tragedy as a sacrifice that man offers to nature in order to help it achieve an adequate appearance. The tragic in man consists in the fact that he can render this service, which lends his being significance, only in death, when he is posited as a sign that is "in itself insignificant = 0." In Hölderlin's view, the conflict between nature and art, whose goal is their reconciliation, comes to the fore in tragedy. In fact, he turns this conflict into the thematic dimension of *Empedocles*, the tragedy he wrote at the same time as these theoretical writings on tragedy. For Hölderlin, Empedocles is "a son of the violent oppositions of nature and art in which the world appeared before his eyes. A man within whom these oppositions are united *so* intimately that they become *one* within him."[5] Empedocles' situation is tragic because he must meet his demise for the sake of the very reconciliation he embodies, indeed, because he embodies it, that is, physically presents it. As "The Ground for Empedocles" elaborates, this reconciliation is recognizable only when what has been bound together in an inner unity is divided through conflict. On the other hand, the physical union can only be merely apparent and temporary and must be sublated, "for otherwise the universal would be lost in the individual, and . . . the life of a world would expire in some particular instance."[6] Empedocles is thus "a victim of his time"[7] whose "passing away," however, enables a "becoming." This fate is not his alone, but rather, as Hölderlin emphasizes, "more or less" the fate of all "tragic figures."[8]

> The presentation of the tragic rests primarily on the following: that the terrible and monstrous—how the god and man mate and how the power of nature and man's innermost depths boundlessly become one in wrath—

> is understood by this boundless union purifying itself through boundless separation.[9]

Hölderlin's "Remarks on 'Oedipus'" and "Remarks on 'Antigone,'" both written in 1803, follow the late hymns, just as the Homburg essays accompany the *Empedocles* tragedy. The definition of tragedy contained in the "Remarks" closely touches upon Hölderlin's early thought on the topic, yet its proximity to the hymns lends it a new meaning. An external sign of this change is already found in the fact that Hölderlin's consideration of the tragic is no longer connected to his own writing, but rather to the translation of Sophocles' tragedies. The tragic solution to the antagonistic relation between nature and art (which Hölderlin's later thought understands in a more absolute fashion as the relation between God and man) is no longer the theme of his own lyric. Admittedly, Hölderlin has not turned away from the tragic dialectic to which he attempted to give form in the *Death of Empedocles*, but in his notion of the relation prevailing between God and man, the tragic is now, so to speak, immanent, as the phrase "divine infidelity" expresses. Hölderlin, observing the matter from the perspective of the philosophy of history, understands both the time in which the action of *Oedipus Rex* is set and his own day as an intermediary time, as the night in which "the god and man, in order that the course of the world has no lacuna and the *memory of the heavenly ones does not expire, express themselves in the all-forgetting form of infidelity*, for it is best to retain and recall divine infidelity."[10] The thematic basis of Hölderlin's late poems is this dialectic of fidelity and infidelity, of remembrance and forgetting. The late poems simultaneously define and fulfill the poet's task in an age when the gods can be near only through their distance. Hölderlin is determined both to hold out in this night of divine distance (which is nevertheless a presence, the only one that does not destroy man) and to prepare the future coming of the gods. This lends his poetry, for example "Celebration of Peace," its utopian structure and its rhythm of extreme tension and expectation, whereby each word braces itself against the longing to which Empedocles surrendered when he threw himself into the Aetna volcano. In Sophoclean tragedy, as well, following Hölderlin's interpretation, the tension is not endured, but brought to a discharge. The chiliastic future of divine proximity prematurely erupts into the present, a present that is not ready for it: A spark leaps over and in the fire that it kindles, night is changed into scorching day. By "interpreting the words of the oracle *too infinitely*,"[11] that is, as a religious demand, and by fulfilling this demand, Oedipus forces a union with God. Yet this "boundless union," as the "Remarks" say, must pass over into a "boundless separation," so that the monstrosity it presents becomes knowable. The forced day tragically turns into an intensified night: into the darkness of the blinded Oedipus.

§ 3 Hegel

> *Tragedy* consists in this, that ethical nature, in order not to become entangled with its inorganic nature, separates the latter from itself as a fate and opposes itself to it; and by acknowledging this fate in the struggle against it, ethical nature is reconciled with the divine being as the unity of both.[1]

Hegel's first interpretation of tragedy is found in the text "On the Scientific Ways of Treating Natural Right," which appeared in 1802–3 in the *Critical Journal of Philosophy*, edited by Schelling and by Hegel himself. Like the journal as a whole, this essay is directed against Kant and Fichte. The struggle that Hegel describes within the field of ethics is, at the same time, a fundamental confrontation between his emerging dialectic (which is first becoming conscious of itself) and the dualistic formalism of the philosophy of his time. Hegel finds fault with the rigid opposition of law and individuality, of universal and particular in Kant's *Critique of Practical Reason* and Fichte's *Foundations of Natural Right*. According to Hegel, Fichte wants "to see every action and the whole existence of the individual as that of an individual who is supervised, known, and regulated by the universal, which stands opposed to him, as well as by abstraction."[2] Hegel counters this Fichtean position with the "absolute idea of ethical life [*Sittlichkeit*],"[3] which contains within itself as "simply identical" the "state of nature" and "the majesty and divinity of the whole state of law which is alien to individuals."[4] Hegel seeks to replace the abstract concept of ethics with a real one that presents the universal and the particular in their identity, for their opposition is caused by formalism's process of abstraction.[5] The real, absolute ethical life, as Hegel understands it, "is immediately the ethical life of the individual; conversely, the essence of the ethical life of the individual [is] simply the real and therefore universal absolute ethical life."[6] Unlike Schelling, Hegel focuses not only on identity, but also on the constant confrontation between the powers grasped in their identity and on the immanent movement of their unity, through which real identity first becomes possible. The opposition between inorganic law and living individuality, between universal and particular, is thus neither excluded nor dismissed; rather, it is sublated into the heart of the concept of identity as a dynamic opposition. As he will later do in *The Phenomenology of Spirit*, Hegel already understands this process as self-division and sacrifice:

> The force of sacrifice lies in viewing [*Anschauen*] and objectifying the entanglement with the inorganic;—this viewing dissolves the entanglement and separates the inorganic, which, having been recognized as such, is taken up into indifference. The living, however, by placing into the inorganic what it knows to be a part of itself and, thereby, sacrificing it to death, has simultaneously recognized the right of the inorganic and purified itself of it.[7]

Hegel equates this process with the tragic process as such and illustrates it through his interpretation of the conclusion of Aeschylus's *Orestia*. The conflict between Apollo and the Eumenides, as the "powers of right in the sphere of difference" (i.e., in the inorganic part of ethics), takes place "in front of the ethical organization, the Athenian people" and concludes with the reconciliation brought about by Pallas Athena. The Eumenides will henceforth be honored as divine powers "so that their savage nature may enjoy (from the altar erected to them in the city below) the sight of Athena enthroned on high on the Acropolis, and thereby be pacified."[8] By interpreting the tragic process as the self-division and self-reconciliation of the ethical nature, Hegel makes his dialectical structure immediately apparent for the first time. In Schelling's definition of the tragic, the dialectical aspect must still be uncovered, for he moves all too quickly toward harmony (which is what Hegel implicitly accuses him of in the preface to the *Phenomenology*). In Hegel, on the contrary, the tragic and the dialectic coincide. This identity is not simply an afterthought, but can be traced back to the origin of both ideas in Hegel as demonstrated by the early text from 1798–1800 known under the title "The Spirit of Christianity and Its Fate." It is significant that the origin of the Hegelian dialectic is a history of the origin of the dialectic as such. Hegel first explains his disagreement with Kantian formalism in the framework of a theological-historical study. This disagreement takes the form of the subject matter itself: the confrontation between Christianity and Judaism. The young Hegel characterizes the spirit of Judaism in terms similar to his later description of Kant's and Fichte's formalism. This spirit is determined by the rigid opposition between the human and the divine, the particular and the universal, life and law, between which no reconciliation is possible. The relation of these terms is that between the ruler and the ruled. The spirit of Christianity stands in opposition to this strictly dualistic spirit. The figure of Jesus bridges the gap between man and God; being at once the Son of God and the Son of man, he incarnates the reconciliation, the dialectical unity of both powers, just as his resurrection mediates between life and death. Jesus replaces the objective command, to which man must submit, with a subjective disposition in which the individual is posited as one with universality. In this early essay, Hegel does not view identity as a stable harmony, any more than he does in his later essay on natural right. Rather, he views identity as possessing an inner movement, which is the very process that will achieve its final form as the dialectic of spirit in the *Phenomenology*. The early text calls the stages of self-division and reconciliation found in the movement from being-in-itself to being-in-and-for-itself "fate" and "love." Judaism, according to Hegel, has no concept of fate, for between man and God there is only a bond of lordship. It is the spirit of Christianity that establishes the possibility of fate. Fate is "nothing foreign like punishment," which belongs to the foreign law, but rather "consciousness of oneself, yet as something hostile."[9] In fate, absolute ethics divides itself within itself. It does not find itself faced with an objective law that it may have transgressed. On the contrary, in the form of fate, absolute ethics has before it the law that it itself established in the course of acting.[10] While an absolute opposition survives punishment in the case of objective law, absolute ethics is offered the possibility of reconciling itself with fate and thus of restoring unity. Hegel's early writing is not merely concerned with the fate of Christianity, as the title provided by the editors maintains, but simultaneously with the genesis of fate in general, which for Hegel coincides with the genesis of the dialectic and, to be precise, commences in the spirit of Christianity. But even here, in the Christian realm, "fate" for Hegel means tragic fate, as can be seen in the definition of tragedy found in the text on natural right, where it signifies the moment of self-division within ethical nature. Among the manuscript pages of Hegel's early writings one finds excerpts concerning *fatum* in the *Iliad*[11] and a clarification, referring to *Macbeth*, of the peculiar nature of fate when it is externalized by an individual subject. After murdering Banquo, Macbeth is not confronted with an alien law existing independently of him; rather, in the form of Banquo's ghost, he faces injured life itself, which is nothing foreign, but his "own forfeited life": "It is now for the first time that the injured life appears as a hostile power against the criminal and mistreats him, just as he has mistreated others. Hence, punishment as fate is the equal reaction of the criminal's own deed, of a power that he himself has armed, of an enemy that he himself created."[12] Because the criminal himself "established this law," "the division he brought about"—unlike what is simply and absolutely divided in the law—can "be united," and "this unification takes place in love."[13] Hegel interprets the fate of Mary Magdalene in this manner, ascribing the guilt for her transgressions entirely to the spirit of Judaism: "the era of her people was one of those in which the beautiful heart could not live without sin, but in this era, as in every other, it could return through love to the most beautiful consciousness."[14] Although Hegel's early text on religion never uses the words "tragic" and "tragedy," it does contain the origin of the definition of the tragic later found in the text on natural right. This origin is at one with the origin of the Hegelian dialectic. For the young Hegel, the tragic process is the dialectic of ethics, which he first sought to demonstrate as the spirit of Christianity and later postulated as the foundation of a new theory of ethics. It is the dialectic of ethics, the dialectic "of the mover of all human things,"[15] that divides itself within itself in fate but then returns to itself in love. In the world of law, on the contrary, the rigid division remains unchanged throughout sin and punishment.

> The proper theme of the original type of tragedy is the divine; not, however, the divine as the content of religious consciousness as such, but as it enters the world and individual action. Yet in this actual appearance, the divine does not lose its substantive character, nor does it see itself there as inverted into the opposite of itself. In this form the spiritual substance of

> willing and accomplishing is the *ethical*. . . . Now, everything that forces its way into the objective and real world is subject to the principle of particularization; consequently the ethical powers, just like the agents, are *differentiated* in their content and their individual appearance. Now if, as dramatic poetry requires, these thus differentiated powers are summoned into appearance as active and are realized as the specific aim of a human "pathos" that passes over into action, then their harmony is cancelled and they come on the scene *opposed to one another* in reciprocal seclusion and isolation. In this event, the individual action will under certain circumstances realize an aim or a character that is one-sidedly isolated in its complete determinacy, and therefore, in the circumstances presupposed, will necessarily rouse against it the opposed "pathos" and, in this way, lead to inevitable conflicts. The original essence of the tragic consists then in the fact that within such a collision each of the opposed sides, if taken by itself, has *justification*; on the other hand, each side can establish the true and positive content of its own aim and character only by negating and infringing upon the equally justified power of the other. Therefore, each side—in its ethical life, and because of it—is equally involved in *guilt*.[16]

Two decades lie between this definition from Hegel's *Aesthetics* and the one found in the essay on natural right. The tragic is still understood as the dialectic of ethical life. But something essential has changed. Admittedly, the tragic hero's fate—the fact that his pathos puts him at the same time in the right and wrong and that he thus incurs guilt precisely through his ethical life—is still seen in a metaphysical context based on the divine entering into a reality that is subject to the principle of particularization. But in contrast to the essay from 1802, this relation has become much looser. The tragic no longer essentially belongs to the idea of the divine, for the divine in religious consciousness lies beyond the tragic. The self-division of the ethical is still unavoidable, but the concrete form of this division is now determined by circumstances surrounding it, rendering it capricious and contingent with respect to content. Unlike Hegel's earlier definition of the tragic, the one he presents in the *Aesthetics* does not appear to be immediately drawn from a philosophical system; rather, corresponding to its position in an aesthetic theory, it strives to encompass the full range of tragic possibilities. From his subsequent remarks in the *Aesthetics* on historical development, it is clear that Hegel only reluctantly concedes the formal expansiveness of his definition and basically would prefer to maintain a single form of tragic collision. The element of chance that has found its way into his definition is obviously derived from the depiction of the tragic found in modernity, whose heroes stand "in the midst of a wide range of more or less accidental relations and conditions within which it is possible to act this way or that."[17] Their behavior is determined by their individual character, which does not necessarily embody an ethical pathos, as was the case in antiquity. For this reason, Hegel accepts modern tragedy only with reservations. Yet even within Greek tragedy, he clearly favors one of the possible tragic collisions, the one that he finds in *Iphigenie in Aulis*, in the *Orestia*, in Sophocles' *Electra*, and most perfectly in *Antigone*, which he calls "the most magnificent and satisfying artwork . . . of all the masterpieces of the ancient and modern world."[18] Hegel's preferred tragic collision is the one between love and law as they meet and clash in the figures of Antigone and Creon. The one form of the tragic that Hegel analyzed in *The Phenomenology of Spirit* therefore still stands behind the apparent indeterminacy of his later definition. One cannot, of course, overlook the fact that in the *Phenomenology*, Sophocles' tragedy is not viewed as tragedy and that Hegel offers no definition of the tragic, for the expressions "tragic" and "tragedy" do not occur in the *Phenomenology*. Rather, in the course of his presentation of the dialectical process of spirit, Hegel reaches the stage of "true spirit," which he defines as "ethics" and splits into two essences: divine law and human law. The first is fulfilled in the woman and the sphere of the family, the latter in the man and the life of the state. In *Antigone*, Hegel sees the collision of these two manifestations of the ethical and, ultimately, the collision of the absolute spirit with itself in the process of returning to itself. Contrary to the *Aesthetics* and in agreement with the early treatise on natural right, the *Phenomenology* places the tragic (of course, without naming it as such) at the center of Hegelian philosophy and interprets it as the dialectic governing ethical life, the spirit in its stage as true spirit. And yet, the proximity between Hegel's early theological text, his essay on natural right, and the *Phenomenology* (and even the *Aesthetics* as its formalized echo) not only reveals their similarities, but also an essential difference, allowing us to deduce a hidden turn in Hegel's conception of the tragic. In the writings prior to the *Phenomenology*, tragedy is the defining trait of an ethical world that is divided within itself in fate and finds reconciliation in love. The world of law, as the opposite of the ethical world, is based on the rigid opposition between the universal and the particular and offers no possibility of the tragic. In the *Phenomenology*, however, the tragic conflict arises precisely between the worlds of law and love. The spirit of Judaism and of formalist ethics, which were once excluded from the tragic realm, appear in the figure of Creon as a tragic hero who is as justified in his actions as his adversary Antigone, who embodies the world of love. This change in Hegel's conception, a change further underscored by Hegel's arguing for Creon's ethical pathos, is related to the change that the significance of the dialectic undergoes. In the years between the text on natural right and the *Phenomenology*, the dialectic ceases to be a historical-theological phenomenon (in the spirit of Christianity) and a scientific postulate (for the reestablishment of an ethical theory) and becomes the law of the world and the method of knowledge. The dialectic, which is also the tragic (and the overcoming of the tragic), thereby goes beyond the limits posited in the two early texts and now also includes the sphere of the law, which was once rigorously differentiated from it. Elevated to the status of a world principle, the dialectic knows no realm that remains closed off to it. Hegel therefore now recognizes the fundamental, tragic conflict as precisely the conflict that necessarily arises between the origin of the dialectic and the realm from which it distanced itself in its coming to be. In Hegel's image of antiquity, the opposition between Judaism and Christianity is sublated.[19] Hegel already prepares for the unification of these once sharply divided worlds in his early theological-historical essay, for even before he names it as such, the dialectic gains its validity behind Hegel's back, so to speak. This can be seen by the curious fact that Hegel seizes upon the same tragedy to characterize both Christianity and Judaism in this essay. A few pages before the analysis of the scene between Macbeth and Banquo's ghost, which shows the dialectic of subjective fate, one finds the sentence that banishes Macbeth into the world of the objective and its harsh oppositions: "The fate of the Jewish people is the fate of Macbeth, who stepped out of nature itself, clung to foreign beings, and thus in their service had to trample and slay everything holy in human nature, had at last to be forsaken by his gods (for they were objects and he their slave), and be crushed to pieces on his faith itself."[20] This twofold interpretation and twofold use of the figure of Macbeth, which itself is evidence of the Hegelian dialectic, anticipates (against the intention of the early work, but in the spirit of his later writings) the synthesis that Hegel achieved in the *Phenomenology* with his interpretation of *Antigone*.[21]

§ 4 Solger

> The tragic principle is when all reality, as the presentation and revelation of the idea, appears contradicting itself and immersing itself in the idea.[1]
>
> In the tragic, the idea as existing is revealed through annihilation; by sublating itself as existence, the idea is present as idea, and both are one and the same. The demise of the idea as existence is its revelation as idea.[2]

Although Solger's *Lectures on Aesthetics*, held in 1819, betray Schelling's influence, they also constitute a decisive turn away from his theory. The Idealist position that can be traced back to Fichte has been shaken. This is clear from the fact that Schelling's notions of "freedom" and "necessity" have been replaced by "idea" and "existence." The hostile power that forces the idea into a tragic process in which it is victorious only through its demise is no longer *fatum* or the necessity of the objective, but human existence itself. The idea has removed itself from the I of the subject (as the seat of freedom) and moved into the realm of the divine. For the young Schelling, the tragic dialectic appears only as a possible struggle between human freedom and the power of the objective. For Solger, the tragic dialectic is a necessary and proper characteristic of man's being: "We are trapped in an existence whose life is turned away from the idea, is lost and void in itself. This existence can obtain meaning, content, and value only if the divine idea reveals itself within it. This revelation, however, is possible only through the sublation of this existence itself."[3] In an essay entitled "Sophocles and Ancient Tragedy," Solger interprets the fate of Antigone and Creon in the same fashion: "Both atone for the split between the eternal and the temporal, a split that can never be reconciled."[4] Yet even for Solger, the tragic ultimately offers consolation: "We know that our demise is not the consequence of fortuitousness, but rather of the fact that existence cannot bear the eternal, for which we are destined. Thus, sacrifice itself is the greatest witness to our being destined for something higher."[5] In Schelling's *Letters*, freedom, as what defines man, is not necessarily first granted to man in his downfall, and in his *Philosophy of Art*, the goal of the conflict between freedom and necessity is their original and divine identity. For Solger, on the contrary, man's inner split—"the fact that man partakes in the loftiest and nevertheless must exist," a circumstance that "produces the truly tragic feeling"—is not sublated, but first experienced in the knowledge that reconciles. This radicalization of the tragic process also characterizes Solger's aesthetics. In Schelling's definition of beauty as the "indifference of freedom and necessity, viewed in a real entity," Solger discovers a tragic dialectic that endures the beautiful as the divine idea. The real (which is where the divine can first be viewed) is for Solger also the annihilation of the divine. Because Solger maintains that something can be known only in its opposite, the idea cannot appear through itself, but must "unfold itself into the oppositions of existence."[6] The idea is thus sublated in the very thing in which it was first realized. From this arises Solger's definition of the tragic. What is "annihilated" in the tragic "is the idea itself, to the extent that it becomes appearance. It is not merely the temporal that meets its demise here; rather, it is precisely the loftiest, the most noble in us that must perish, for the idea cannot exist without being its opposite."[7]

§ 5 Goethe

> Everything tragic is based upon an irreconcilable [*unausgleichbar*] opposition. As soon as a reconciliation [*Ausgleichung*] sets in or becomes possible, the tragic disappears.[1]

The formal character of Goethe's remark, which Chancellor von Müller reports on June 6, 1824, is notable. For Goethe, intuition [*Anschauung*] and theory are usually one and the same. Yet two things help him achieve here this acute ability to abstract: the distance he takes in confronting the problem of the tragic and his determination to grant this problem no place in the concrete realms of his being. Goethe can thus recognize an essential trait of the tragic, one that is concealed by Schelling's and even Hegel's Idealist systems and one that alienates him most: the tragic conflict "does not allow a resolution."[2] In 1831, Goethe mentioned to Zelter that he was "not born to be a tragic poet, for my nature is conciliatory." For Goethe, the irreconcilable that characterizes the purely tragic case seems to be "fully absurd."[3] The definition of the tragic that Goethe expressed to Eckermann in 1827 and intended as a critique of Hegel's interpretation of *Antigone* possesses a formal expansiveness that had to be a bit odd, even for Goethe himself. He imposes the restriction that the conflict, in order to be tragic, must "have a genuine, natural foundation beneath it" and must be "a genuinely tragic foundation." Eckermann may bear the blame for this flawed reasoning. Or perhaps it betrays Goethe's own embarrassment in the face of the problem of the tragic, as he confided to Zelter. There are, however, initial signs in Goethe of a more concrete definition of the tragic:

Vom tragisch Reinen stellen wir euch dar
Des düstern Wollens traurige Gefahr;
Der kräftige Mann, voll;
Trieb und willevoll,
Er kennt sich nicht, er weiß nicht, was er soll.

[From the tragically pure we present you
The sad danger of dark desire;
The powerful man, full;
Driven and willful,
He doesn't know himself, he doesn't know what he ought to.[4]]

The muse speaks these lines in the drama *Prologue to the Opening of the Berlin Theater in May 1821.* The verse summarizes thoughts that Goethe had already developed in "Shakespeare and No End" (1813). In this essay, Goethe traces the tragic elements back to the "disparity between 'ought' and 'desire' that everyone possesses."[5] He thus arrives at a differentiation of the tragic in antiquity, modernity, and Shakespeare, who combines the two forms of the tragic. For Goethe, two things are essential: The tragic conflict should not solely take place between the tragic hero and the outer world, nor should it be rooted in the superior power of the divine or fate, for "ohne Zeus und Fatum, spricht mein Mund,/Ging Agamemnon, ging Achill zugrund [without Zeus and *fatum*, my mouth says,/Both Agamemnon and Achilles met their end]."[6] Rather, the scene of the tragic conflict is man himself, in whom "ought" and "desire" diverge and threaten to burst the unity of the I. The banal disparity of not desiring what one should or of desiring what one should not is, of course, not tragic. On the contrary, what is tragic is the blindness in which one, deceived about the aim of his "ought," must desire what he is not allowed to desire. This decisive addition to Goethe's definition of the tragic—that the irreconcilable opposition divides what is one—appears in another form in his review of Manzoni's *The Count of Carmagnola*, written a year earlier. Goethe calls the subject matter lying at the heart of the opposition between the *condottiere* Carmagnola and the Venetian senate "completely pregnant, tragic, irreconcilable," for here, "two incompatible, contradictory groups believe that they can be united in and dedicated to a common cause."[7] Even if it were irresolvable, the mere conflict between Carmagnola and the senate is not tragic. Rather, what is tragic is the fact that they are united in *one common* purpose. Alongside these definitions of the tragic derived from Goethe's discussion of foreign literature, there is another, which can be said to represent Goethe's most proper feelings:

> The fundamental motive of all tragic situations is the act of departing, which requires neither poison nor dagger, neither spear nor sword. To be more or less compelled to part from an accustomed, desired, and upright situation by a powerful force that is more or less hated is also a variation of this theme.[8]

Written in 1821 along with the *Prologue to the Opening of the Berlin Theater*, this sentence from *Wilhelm Tischbein's Idylls* gives the lie to the assertion that the problem of the tragic was essentially foreign to Goethe. The reason why Goethe did not feel he was born to be a tragic poet was not his unfamiliarity with the tragic, but his intimate familiarity with it. Only the violent intensification of the tragic that the dramatist produces on the stage with violence and, indeed, pleasure would alienate Goethe. In real-life events, Goethe felt the tragic deeply and painfully. He retrieves the tragic element from the death of the tragic hero (whose authors are compulsion and violence, whose emblems are poison and dagger) and places it into the act of departing from a beloved one or a beloved situation. Nothing would be more erroneous than to see in Goethe a trivialization of the tragic problem or, indeed, a confusing of the tragic with what is only sorrowful. The significance of departing for Goethe can be measured by the position that the present and the moment assume in his poetry, let alone in the works whose theme is departure. Goethe could call the act of departing the fundamental motive of all tragic situations because he was aware of its dialectical structure. Departure is oneness, whose only theme is separation; it is proximity that now looks only into the distance, that strives for distance, regardless of how hateful it may be; it is closeness, which separation itself, the death of closeness, consummates as departure.

§ 6 Schopenhauer

> It is the antagonism of the will with itself which is here [in tragedy] most completely unfolded at the highest grade of its objectivity, and which comes into fearful prominence. This antagonism becomes visible in the suffering of mankind which is produced, in part, by chance and error; and these stand forth as the rulers of the world, personified as fate through their insidiousness, which appears almost like purpose and intention. This antagonism also proceeds, in part, from mankind itself through the conflicting efforts of the will on the part of individuals, through the wickedness and perversity of most. It is one and the same will, living and appearing in them all, whose phenomena fight with one another and tear one another to pieces.[1]

> Everything tragic, regardless of the form in which it appears, receives its characteristic tendency toward the sublime from the dawning of the knowledge that the world and life can afford us no true satisfaction, and are therefore not worth our attachment to them. In this the tragic spirit consists; accordingly, it leads to resignation.[2]

The World as Will and Representation first appeared in 1819 in an edition that remained unnoticed for a long time. Solger held his *Lectures on Aesthetics* in the same year, though they were first published posthumously a decade later. Schopenhauer's definition of the tragic has much in common with Solger's. For Schopenhauer, the tragic process is also the autosublation of what founds the world. But whereas for Solger the idea reveals itself for the first time as idea in its demise (a Schellingesque thought), for Schopenhauer, the self-negation of the will has its value in itself. And while Solger's interpretation of the tragic is still entirely developed out of the duality of idea and existence, Schopenhauer's definition has only the concept of will at its base. In the concept of will, Schopenhauer found the answer to Faust's inquiry into "what holds the world together in its inmost being" (the verses are the motto of the second book); the will is "the thing-in-itself, the source of all phenomena." Schopenhauer can therefore call the will's "self-knowledge the sole event in-itself"[3] and equate it with the tragic process. Whereas the tragic process for Solger takes place in the entrance of the divine idea into existence, for Schopenhauer, this occurs in the objectification of the will. The universe consists of gradations in the will's objectification; a series of stages leads from the inorganic through plants and animals to man. "Considered purely in itself," the will "is devoid of knowledge and is only a blind, irresistible urge." Yet in the ascending forms of its objectification, the will "obtains knowledge of its own willing and what it wills through the addition of the world of representation, developed for its service."[4] The sole goal of art is the communication of this knowledge.[5] The process of objectification and self-knowledge thus culminates in man and art. From these two points of view, Schopenhauer's description of tragedy interprets the tragic as the self-destruction and self-negation of the will. In the conflicts that constitute the plot of tragedy (regardless of whether they occur between man and fate or between man and man), Schopenhauer sees the will's diverse manifestations battling against each other and, thus, the battle of the will against itself. This tragic dialectic of the will is completed not within the thematic space of tragedy, but only through its effect upon the spectators and readers, that is, in the knowledge that tragedy conveys. Yet this knowledge, according to Schopenhauer, proceeds "originally from the will itself"; knowledge "belongs to the inner being of the higher stages of the will's objectification" and is "a means of preserving both the individual and the species. . . . Destined to serve the will, to fulfill its goals, knowledge remains almost throughout entirely subordinate to its service. This is the case with all animals and almost all men." Knowledge can, however, sometimes "withdraw itself" from "this servitude" and, "freed from all the aims of the will," establish art as "a clear mirror of the world."[6] Therefore, the possibility contained in all art—that knowledge, which is derived from the will and should serve it, turns against it—is realized in tragedy. The presentation of the will's self-destruction engenders in the spectator the knowledge that life, as the object and objectivity of this will, "is not worth our attachment to it" and thus leads the will to resignation. In resignation, the will, whose manifestation is man, sublates itself in a dual dialectic. The will not only turns against itself in the knowledge that it "turned on like a light,"[7] but also brings about this knowledge through the tragic action whose sole hero is the will, the will that destroys itself.

§ 7 Friedrich Theodor Vischer

> Two elements . . . form the true concept of tragic fate: the absolute and the subject. Both stand in relationship to one another, whereby the latter, the subject, owes his existence, his abilities, and his greatness to the absolute. The subject thereby appears as a significant power. But he only appears thus; the tragic demonstrates that he owes his greatness to a higher power and this greatness, when compared with that of the higher power, is only a relative greatness, suffering from weaknesses and frailty. . . . But because divine sublimity is revealed in the demise of human sublimity, the pain in the spectator passes over into a feeling of reconciliation.[1]

Vischer's interpretation of the tragic from the treatise *On the Sublime and the Comical* (1837) recurs in scarcely amended form in his *Aesthetics*, published between 1847 and 1857. This interpretation is dependent on Hegel to a much higher degree and in a wholly different manner than Hegel influenced Kierkegaard's thought or Schopenhauer Nietzsche's *The Birth of Tragedy*. From the very beginning, Nietzsche and Kierkegaard programmatically turn their backs on what shaped them most and thereby arrive at something new. Vischer, on the contrary, gradually frees himself from Hegel during his long work on the *Aesthetics*; only in 1873, in his second *Critique of My Aesthetics*, does he manage to come to the following decision: "I surrender the entire method of the Hegelian conceptual movement, which is intended to be the immanent and logical movement of the matter itself."[2] Vischer himself admits that he "did not have a basic idea for a new philosophical structure, not even of its essential elements."[3] Nevertheless, already at the very beginning of his thought there are deviations from Hegel that one can trace back to deep-seated differences, differences that Vischer himself was not always conscious of and that lie concealed behind the words.[4] Even if they are of secondary importance, these differences affect his interpretation of the tragic. When Vischer was writing *On the Sublime and the Comical*, only the first volume of Hegel's *Lectures on Aesthetics* had appeared. Vischer therefore uses Hegel's *Aesthetics* as the basis for his concept of the beautiful, while *The Phenomenology of Spirit* grounds his concept of the tragic. On the face of it, the originality of Vischer's definition of the tragic lies in his taking Hegel's interpretation of tragedy from the process of absolute spirit and transferring it to the system of the beautiful. And this originality is to be found more in the context than in the text itself. The reason for Vischer's insertion of the tragic into the dialectical movement of the beautiful lies, however, neither in this necessary transferal nor merely in his attempt to lead Hegel's aesthetics (which were not dialectical enough for him) in this direction so as to complete them. Rather, the reason is found in the decisive sentence from *On the Sublime and the Comical*: "the beautiful must show us not only the *resolved* contradiction, but also the *contradiction* that it resolves."[5] The motivating force behind this thought is Vischer's desire to pay more attention than Hegel did to chance (as one of the hypostatic elements of the beautiful) and, therefore, to the individual and the comical. Following Ewald Volhard, this attentiveness to chance comes from the fact that Vischer no longer understands the fundamental concept of his and Hegel's systems—the idea—as a process, but as static, whereby being and becoming, spirit and reality, are once again, and against Hegel, torn apart. Reality thus appears in its capriciousness. Vischer's long process of detaching himself from Hegel, which culminates in his surrendering the Hegelian method of conceptual movement, is thereby introduced into his aesthetics from the very beginning. The text *On the Sublime and the Comical* is included in Vischer's *Aesthetics* as its first part, bearing the title *The Metaphysics of the Beautiful*. After reducing the beautiful to its two elements, the idea and the image, whose harmonious unity constitutes the beautiful, this text deals with the beautiful "in the conflict of its elements," a phrase that corresponds to the above-quoted programmatic sentence. Vischer designates the sublime as the first contrast within the beautiful (the second will be the comical). In the sublime, "the idea stands in a negative relation to objectivity; the absolute appears, raised above every immediate existence."[6] Within the sublime, Vischer further differentiates between an objective and a subjective sublime, whose dialectical unity, the sublime of the subject-object, he defines as the tragic. Vischer thereby arrives at Hegel's interpretation of tragedy in the *Phenomenology*, which he adopts in the new context produced by his explanation of the dialectic of the beautiful. Whereas Hegel's train of thought concerning the "true spirit" (which Hegel defines as ethical life) leads directly to the form of the tragic illustrated by *Antigone*, Vischer divides his section on the tragic into three parts. Vischer thus emphasizes an essential element in the tragic dialectic that, for Hegel, arises out of the subject matter itself. In the first stage, the subject falls prey to the absolute, which is "the obscure foundation of an infinite natural power."[7] In the second stage, where the "truly tragic" begins, according to Vischer, fate "as justice" holds sway.[8] Only in the third stage, which corresponds to Hegel's interpretation in the *Phenomenology* and for Vischer is the "purest form of the tragic," does the absolute spirit appear "as the purely spiritual unity of all ethical truths and laws," while the subject "has made *one* of these truths his own pathos."[9] Here, the conflict between the subject and the absolute finally becomes dialectical. The pathos of the subject proves him to be at once right and wrong: right in his ethical life, and wrong insofar as he is one-sided and infringes upon other ethical laws. Following the formulation of the 1837 text, the subject owes its existence and greatness to the absolute, which is ethics in its totality. Precisely because of this debt to the absolute, the subject must also meet its demise and, thus, as an individual among individuals, finds itself faced with another concrete form of ethical life. In his *Aesthetics*, Vischer interprets the tragic dialectic of the subject that is destroyed by itself, by the very fact of being an individual (as in Hebbel and later in Nietzsche), as the guilt [*Verschuldung*] of individuation. The sublime in the subject is annihilated not only because it is merely a fraction, but also because it is "a fraction that is bent on dividing the whole."[10] From the perspective of the absolute, the tragic process is the battle that the ethical life wages against itself in the form of its opposing particulars. To this extent, the tragic process is also a dialectical process, in which, unlike Schopenhauer's will and like Solger's divine idea and Nietzsche's Dionysus, the absolute reveals itself precisely in its indestructibility.

§ 8 Kierkegaard

The tragic is the suffering contradiction.[1]

The tragic perspective sees the contradiction and despairs of a way out.[2]

Kierkegaard's definition of the tragic is related to Goethe's for two reasons: first, because it gets by without any determinations of content and, second, because the formal perspective of both authors, which is not guided by the will to a system, inevitably seizes upon an identical dialectic of the tragic. And yet Kierkegaard's definition differs from Goethe's in two areas that enable a more precise view both of the structure of the tragic and of its status in Kierkegaard's thought. While Goethe speaks of an "opposition," Kierkegaard (following the diction of Hegel's *Logic*) chooses the concept of "contradiction" (*Modsigelse*). Kierkegaard thus expresses the predetermined unity of the colliding powers, a unity that makes their conflict tragic. What Goethe only later adds to his definition of the tragic in its application to Manzoni's *Carmagnola*[3] is already intended by Kierkegaard in the word *Modsigelse* and expressly stated in *Either/Or*: "For the tragic conflict to have genuine depth, the conflicting forces must be of the same kind."[4] The second difference is more important. Although Goethe mentioned to Zelter that the irreconcilable seems absurd to him, he accepted the "irreconcilable opposition" upon which the tragic rests as an objective fact, just as he viewed the reconciliation through which the tragic disappears as independent of the subject. For Kierkegaard, on the contrary, the tragic contradiction's lack of a way out does not reside in reality, but merely in one's *perspective* on the situation. Thus, if one cannot force one's way out, one still has the possibility of sublating the contradiction into a higher perspective, where it no longer is a matter of finding a way out. This mode of overcoming the tragic is always already contained within Idealist interpretations since Schelling. Even resignation, which Schopenhauer views as the goal of this overcoming, has the same teleological dignity that is proper to Schelling's assertion of freedom or Solger's knowledge of the divine idea. Kierkegaard, on the contrary, separates the redemptive element from the tragic and in this respect is also the religious precursor of a nonreligious thought. He thereby prepares an analysis of the tragic that is free from all metaphysical meaning. For Kierkegaard, this means that the tragic can only be something preliminary. The path of his existential thought no longer allows for a system and severely condemns the element of Hegel that is, according to its essence, objective and procedural. Corresponding to the idea of the qualitative leap, Kierkegaard's thought takes various stages of existence as its foundation. The tragic is therefore restricted to one of these stages, the ethical, which it is essential to overcome. The concept of the tragic disappears from Kierkegaard's writings after 1846 and in the early works is almost never considered for its own sake; rather, it is contrasted to its opposing concepts from the religious stage. *Fear and Trembling* thus raises Abraham, "the knight of faith," above the "tragic hero" Agamemnon. Following Hegel's footsteps, the young Kierkegaard deprives the "inescapable contradiction" of its radicality (as is Agamemnon's case in the ethical sphere) so as to contrast more powerfully the religious paradox of Abraham's fate with this contradiction: "The tragic hero surrenders the certain for the sake of what is even more certain, and the spectators' eyes rest upon him without a worry."[5] After Kierkegaard's theory of the stages of existence has been elaborated, the tragic and its possible overcoming are viewed differently. In the context of the definition quoted at the beginning, Kierkegaard writes in *Concluding Unscientific Postscript* (1846) that despair knows no way out, it "does not know the contradiction cancelled, and ought therefore to apprehend the contradiction tragically, which is precisely the way to its healing. Humor has its justification precisely in its tragic side, in the fact that it reconciles itself to the pain that despair seeks to abstract from, although it knows no way out."[6] Humor already appeared in Kierkegaard's dissertation as "the viewpoint of the religious." Along the path of his thought and life, the tragic is replaced by humor, which now is defined as "the border between the ethical and the religious." Kierkegaard therefore appears to be less a theoretician of the tragic than of its opposing concepts: irony, humor, and the comical, whose affinity with the tragic became clearer to him the more he freed himself from it. Kierkegaard has his pseudonym Frater Taciturnus declare in the postscript to Quidam's tale of woe: "The matter is not so bad for me; I sit here entirely pleased with my calculations, and see both the comical and the tragic."[7] This derisive distance from oneself can scarcely conceal the fact that for Kierkegaard, the concept of the tragic was not a mere aid in grasping the religious, but the key to his own particular problem of suffering, whose (initially ironic) solution he hoped to obtain from this higher stage. This importance of the tragic is proven by the sketch of an Antigone tragedy in *Either/Or* under which the traditional version of Kierkegaard's life story has been subsumed. Oedipus dies without his sins coming to light, and Antigone (who already intuited these sins while he was alive, but remained silent and lapsed into depression) is "fatally in love." To be able to declare her love to her beloved, Antigone would have to entrust him with the secret of her melancholy—yet were she to do this, she would lose him. Kierkegaard writes: "Only in the moment of her death can Antigone confess the fervency of her love; only in the moment when she no longer belongs to him can she confess that she belongs to him."[8] Kierkegaard compares her secret to Epaminodas's arrow, which he left in the wound after the battle because he knew that he would die if the arrow were removed. In the same way, Kierkegaard's knowledge of his father's youthful folly and his awareness of his own transgression stood as an obstacle between him and Regina. Kierkegaard's tragic fate was the one endured by Antigone. He had to make Regina unhappy by breaking off their engagement; this was his only hope for making her happy.[9] Kierkegaard interprets both Antigone's and his own melancholy in this image, whose dialectical meaning is that precisely through the emancipation from what brings death, death is brought about. The biblical thorn in one's flesh became for Kierkegaard the tragic emblem of his life.[10]

§ 9 Hebbel

> Drama presents the life process in itself. It does so . . . in the sense that it recalls for us the alarming relation in which the individual, who has been discharged from the original nexus, stands opposed to the whole of which he still remains a part, despite his inconceivable freedom.[1]

> Art . . . was able to dissolve isolation again and again through the excess implanted in isolation itself and to free the idea from its defective form. Guilt lies in excess. The isolated one is excessive only because he, as imperfect, has no claim to permanence and thus must work toward his own *destruction.* Therefore, reconciliation also lies in excess, insofar as one can ask for reconciliation in the realm of art. This guilt is an absolutely original one that cannot be separated from the concept of man and scarcely falls into his consciousness. It is posited with life itself.[2]

Numerous passages from Hebbel's diary demonstrate that the word "drama" in these sentences from *My Word on Drama* (1843) is to be understood as tragedy and the word "art" as tragic art. In his diary, Hebbel writes: "Life is the great river, individuals are drops, and tragic individuals are pieces of ice that have to be melted again. For this to be possible, the ice blocks must destroy and crush each other."[3] Just like pieces of ice, the tragic hero removes himself from his original context, exceeds his limits, and thus provokes the resistance of another. Although his metamorphosis into a rigid, isolated entity arises not merely from his own will, but also from the objective life process, the tragic hero, through his changed form, contradicts the idea of a flowing life and therefore must perish. It is not this violent force that directly destroys the tragic hero, but rather another individual, one who shares the tragic hero's fate by paying for his victory over the hero with his own downfall. Both thereby return to the whole from which they seceded. As delineated by the text cited at the beginning of this section, Hebbel's metaphorical use of a natural process illustrates that the tragic is not to be separated from the essence of man. According to Hebbel, man necessarily turns against the totality of life by obeying its law of individuation; he is destroyed by his own nature, by being what he is. For Hebbel, "how the hero meets his demise, whether in an excellent or reprehensible effort, is in no way trivial. On the contrary, if the most deeply shocking image is to come into being, it is necessary that the former and not the latter take place."[4] This conception of the tragic, whose dialectical essence is perfectly clear, is shaped by Hegel and Solger.[5] In the tragic, Schelling saw the battle of subjective freedom against objective necessity in which freedom proves itself through its demise, while the young Hegel saw here the self-division and self-reconciliation of ethics. Yet it is Solger who first formulates the thought that the tragic can be traced back to the incompatibility between idea and existence, to the divine entering into reality's oppositions, which annihilate as well as reveal the divine. Indeed, Hegel adopts this same motif from Solger for his *Aesthetics*, which, in contrast to the *Phenomenology* and the essay on natural right, explains the tragic as the manifestation of the divine in the world of particularization. Like Schopenhauer and later Nietzsche, Hebbel, following in Hegel's footsteps, considers the principle of individuation to be the source of the tragic. Yet Hebbel's view of the tragic differs from both Hegel's and Nietzsche's forms of optimism, which respectively rest upon faith in the course of spirit and faith in the power of the Dionysian, as well as from Schopenhauer's pessimism, which draws from itself its consolation in resignation. Hebbel marks a turning point in the intellectual history of the nineteenth century. He still follows the metaphysical path of Idealism, yet without knowing the meaning that once served as a guide for that path. Hebbel writes in his diary: "Life is a frightful necessity that must be accepted in good faith, and yet no one comprehends this necessity."[6] Another passage states: "Modern fate is the silhouette of God, of the inconceivable, and of the ungraspable."[7] Hebbel "never found an answer" to the question as to why the individual must be separated and torn from the totality of life, "and no one who seriously poses the question ever will."[8] Because "drama, together with the mystery of the world, is lost in one and the same night,"[9] the tragic in man is intensified in a twofold fashion. Hegel's tragic hero—whose pathos one-sidedly represents the ethical life—assumes guilt only in the face of other embodiments of the ethical; he is not guilty in the face of the ethical life itself. In Hebbel, on the contrary, man becomes guilty in a Kafkaesque process that cannot be rationally resolved and in the face of a life power that he neither recognizes nor comprehends. Hebbel's deviation from Hegel (whose concept of guilt Hebbel still believes he shares) becomes evident in his interpretation of *Antigone*.[10] Hebbel does not view Creon as an equally justified tragic hero. He therefore has Antigone meet her demise through an assumption of guilt, not in the face of the law, but against the totality of life, from which she has removed herself as an individual.[11] In accordance with Hebbel's radicalization of guilt, reconciliation is impossible "within the range of an individual reconciliation [*Ausgleichung*]," that is, in tragedy itself.[12] Even in the realm of meaning that becomes visible beyond the work itself, Hebbel leaves behind the viewpoint of German Idealism. For Solger, the fact that existence cannot bear the eternal serves as evidence of its being destined for the eternal, while Schopenhauer affirms the autosublation of the will in resignation. For Hebbel, on the contrary, tragic art "destroys the individual life in the face of the idea" and thus "lifts itself above individual life." Tragic art is, therefore, "the luminous lightning bolt of human consciousness that . . . can illuminate only what it consumes."[13] The meaning that tragedy makes known in annihilation is itself annihilated in this very knowledge. Hebbel's "pantragic" culminates in the tragedy of tragic art. Admittedly, the now inapplicable metaphysical justification of the tragic is occasionally replaced by one based on the philosophy of history, which Hebbel also adopts from Hegel, for whom the process of spirit is simultaneously world history.[14] This process of spirit is secularized into a merely historical process in the definition of the tragic act that Hebbel provides in the preface to *Mary Magdalene*. Hebbel calls Judith's act "tragic," that is, "an act that, because of its world-historical purpose, is in itself *necessary*, but at the same time one that *destroys* the individual entrusted with its execution because it partially violates the ethical law."[15] It is no accident that this sentence is located in the very preface that attempts to justify "bourgeois tragedy" [*bürgerliches Trauerspiel*]. Both points indicate the path that will lead Hebbel from Idealism to sociological historicism. As the sketch for a Napoleon tragedy demonstrates, even the term "isolation" (which Hebbel uses in place of "particularization" and "*principium individuationis*" as the fundamental concept of his interpretation of the tragic) had assumed from early on a concrete, social meaning in addition to a metaphysical one. In 1838, Hebbel writes in his diary that Napoleon's mistake lies in the fact "that he believes he has the power" to be able to carry out "everything through himself, through his own person." This mistake is "based entirely in his great individuality and, in any case, is the mistake of a god." Hebbel, however, decisively turns this characteristic, which could also be that of Holofernes, in a historical- sociological direction by adding that this flaw is "enough to topple him . . . especially in our age, when it is less the individual than the mass that asserts itself."[16]

§ 10 Nietzsche

> Those who have never had the experience of having to see at the same time that they also longed to transcend all seeing will scarcely be able to imagine how definitely and clearly these two processes coexist and are felt at the same time, as one contemplates the tragic myth. But all truly aesthetic spectators will confirm that among the peculiar effects of tragedy this coexistence is the most remarkable. Now transfer this phenomenon of the aesthetic spectator into an analogous process in the tragic artist, and you will have understood the genesis of the *tragic myth*. With the Apollonian art sphere he shares the complete pleasure in mere appearances and in seeing, yet at the same time he negates this pleasure and finds a still higher satisfaction in the destruction of the visible world of mere appearance.[1]

The pathos of *The Birth of Tragedy* (1870–71) lies in its resistance to Schopenhauer's theory of resignation, but the text itself is shaped down to its last detail by Schopenhauer's system. Although Schopenhauer's influence appears in crucial moments only negatively, it reveals itself not only in the interpretation of music, but also in that of the tragic process and, indeed, in the two fundamental concepts of this early text. Schopenhauer's concepts "will" and "representation" can be seen as forebears of Nietzsche's artistic principles "Dionysian" and "Apollonian." Nietzsche rediscovered the originally blind drive of the will in Dionysus's world of revelry and the visibility and self-knowledge of representation in Apollo's world of dreams and images, whose imperative for humanity is "know thyself."[2] Schopenhauer's metaphysical concepts thus become aesthetic concepts, just as metaphysics as such appears in Nietzsche in the form of aesthetics: "Existence and the world are justified only as an aesthetic phenomenon." Nietzsche accordingly demands that the tragic myth be explained through the aesthetic sphere.[3] Nietzsche's interpretation of the tragic appears to proceed from his interpretation of Attic tragedy, which he understands as the reconciliation of the two artistic principles that continuously fought against each another in the preceding periods of Greek art, as "the Dionysian chorus which discharges itself always anew in an Apollonian world of images."[4] But Nietzsche's interpretation also perfectly reflects, although inverted, the image Schopenhauer sketched of the tragic process. Just as Schopenhauer viewed the conflicting powers of tragedy as manifestations of the one will, Nietzsche maintains that up until Euripides, Dionysus "never ceased to be the tragic hero; all the celebrated figures of the Greek stage—Prometheus, Oedipus, etc.—are mere masks of this original hero, Dionysus."[5] Dionysus's mythical fate of being torn to pieces is celebrated anew in every tragedy. Nietzsche understands this fate as the symbol of individuation; in the tragic hero one can see "the god experiencing in himself the agonies of individuation."[6] Dionysus's fate thereby corresponds to the fate that befalls the will in Schopenhauer's notion of tragedy: The individuals in whom the will appears tear themselves apart. The affinity between Nietzsche's concept of the "Apollonian" and Schopenhauer's "representation" reveals itself precisely in this correspondence. Whereas Schopenhauer's will objectifies itself on the highest level in tragedy, Nietzsche describes the dramatic dialogue as "the objectification of a Dionysian condition." In both concepts, the Apollonian and representation, individuation is placed in opposition to an original oneness (the Dionysian or the will). This comparison, however, also brings to light the decisive difference between Nietzsche's and Schopenhauer's conceptions of the tragic. In Schopenhauer's notion of the tragic process, the will both sublates itself (through its manifestations tearing themselves apart) and effectuates a turning away from itself, that is, resignation (through the knowledge engendered in the spectators). For Nietzsche, on the contrary, Dionysus emerges from his dismemberment in the process of individuation as one who is powerful and indestructible, which is precisely the "metaphysical consolation" that tragedy offers. Nietzsche confronts Schopenhauer's negative dialectic with a positive dialectic that is reminiscent of Schelling's interpretation in the *Letters*. Whereas the will negates itself in its objectification as appearance, the Dionysian (despite its pleasure in the Apollonian world of mere appearance, which is its objectification) affirms itself precisely by negating this pleasure and mere appearance and by taking a still greater pleasure in the destruction of the visible world of mere appearance. Art is thus no longer the clear mirror in which the world of individuation passes judgment on the will. Rather, art is a sign that individuation represents both "the prime cause of evil" and "the joyous hope that the spell of individuation may be broken—the augury of a restored oneness."[7]

§ 11 Simmel

> In contrast to a sorrowful fate or one whose destructive force is external, we characterize a tragic fate as follows: The destructive powers directed toward a being arise from the deepest strata of this very being and, with its destruction, a fate takes place that is moored in the being itself and, so to speak, is the logical development of the very structure with which the being constructed its own positivity.[1]

The tragic appeared in the metaphysical and aesthetic systems of German Idealism as their central dialectical process; the philosophers of the post-Idealist era displace this process into a dialectic of concepts and ideas in whose name they terminate systematic thinking. For Kierkegaard, it is the stages of existence that can no longer systematically be brought into line with thought; for Nietzsche it is the sphere of the aesthetic. In Georg Simmel's work, the concept of the tragic appears in the context of the concept of life. The same applies to Dilthey, who makes the following note in his posthumously published sketch *Historical Consciousness and Worldviews* under the title "The Fundamental Point of the Tragic": "Thinking: relation of components. This in opposition to the life concept of the whole. The tragedy is, however, that we can have this life concept only in this form."[2] On various occasions, and perhaps independently of Dilthey, Simmel demonstrated his notion of the tragic dialectic through examples taken from concrete life situations: Life can be grasped only in a form in which it is no longer grasped as life, whereby other elements that are both necessary and contrary to life replace the element of the concept. The essay "The Concept and the

Tragedy of Culture," written in 1912, is based on this tragic dialectic. The essay takes as its starting point the poured-out spirit, so to speak, which has become an object and "opposes flowing liveliness, inner self-responsibility, and the changing tensions of the subjective soul. As spirit, it is most inwardly bound to spirit, but precisely for this reason it experiences countless tragedies due to the deep formal conflict between subjective life, which is restless but temporally finite, and its contents, which, once created, are immobile, but eternally valid."[3] Often it is "as if the soul's productive liveliness [*Bewegtheit*] would die from its own product."[4] And "thus the tragic situation arises that culture, already in its first moments of being, holds within itself the very form of its contents, which is determined, as through an immanent unavoidability, to distract and burden its inner essence (the path of the soul from itself as incomplete, to itself as complete) and to make this essence baffled and discordant."[5] In just this manner Simmel writes in his diary that the "tragic fundamental phenomenon" of marriage lies in "life creating a form that is indispensable for it but, through the mere fact of being a form, is hostile to life's liveliness and individuality."[6] The life concept "individuality" returns in another sentence from Simmel's diary that takes as its object the tragic aspect of love: "Love is kindled only by individuality and falls to pieces through the insurmountability of individuality."[7] A further passage describes "the true and great tragic situation of the ethical: when one does not have the right to what one has as a duty."[8] The central concept of Simmel's philosophy has already been abandoned here; the tragic has been completely raised above the fundamental idea, which now in the post-Idealist era easily adopts the claim to totality, against which this idea revolts, from the vanquished systematic thinking. It is precisely the contestable vagueness and emptiness of his life concept, together with his dialectical form of thought (indebted to Hegel), that made a glance into the phenomenon of the tragic possible for Simmel. This is clear even in the initially cited text, which is placed almost incidentally in the essay "The Concept and the Tragedy of Culture." This glance permits the various tragic phenomena not only to be understood as tragic in their structurally common features, but also to be left untouched in their particularity. Like Goethe and Kierkegaard before him, but in a more legitimate manner, Simmel viewed the tragic from its own point of view, one that admittedly still belongs to human representation, but is related to nothing but the tragic itself. Despite its linguistic formulation, Simmel's definition of the tragic is in fact the only one that may support an interpretation that wants to find in tragedies forms of the tragic and not the mirror image of one's own philosophical statements.

§ 12 Scheler

> The "conflict" that reigns within positive values and their bearers is tragic.[1]

> It is tragic in the most pronounced sense . . . when one and the same power allows a thing to realize a high, positive value (of itself or of another thing) and, in the process of effectuating this, causes the destruction of just this thing as a value bearer.[2]

Scheler's interpretation of the tragic in the essay "On the Phenomenon of the Tragic" (1915) betrays the influence of Simmel's analysis, but exists wholly within the context of the book he published in 1913, *Formalism in Ethics and Non-Formal Ethics of Value.* The book's main goal is to overcome phenomenologically the Kantian system in the field of ethics. In its point of departure the book admittedly goes back to life philosophy, yet reproaches Kant for believing that life "is not at all a basic phenomenon."[3] Precisely because life, as an indivisible unity, is a basic phenomenon, phenomenology considers its task to consist of tearing down the barrier between subject and object. Thus, Scheler also seeks to overcome the difference that critical philosophy posited between the a priori world of the formal and the world of matter. To ground an ethics that is simultaneously materialistic and a priori, Scheler sketches a phenomenology of value qualities that, according to him, present "a special domain of *objectivities.*"[4] The most important element of this phenomenology is Scheler's assumption of positive and negative values, as well as higher and lower ones, whose existence should lie "in the essence of values." The basis of Scheler's interpretation of the tragic is thus formed. In Idealist systems, the tragic appeared as the dialectical process of self-destruction or of self-confirmation through self-destruction, a process that assumed the highest value: Schelling's freedom, Solger's divine idea, Schopenhauer's will, or Nietzsche's Dionysian principle. Because Scheler's phenomenology no longer admits a highest value, but differentiates between positive and negative, higher and lower values, the tragic makes its appearance as a conflict between positive values and, in the ideal scenario, between positive values of an equally high degree.[5] In a schema roughly corresponding to Vischer's triadic structure, in which the adversary of subjective ethics first appears as fate, then as justice, and finally, establishing the purest form of the tragic, as the totality of ethical truths, Scheler also traces an intensification in the tragic phenomenon that reaches a conclusion only beyond the lofty identity of the values battling one another. This conclusion occurs when "it is one and the same power that allows a thing to realize a high, positive value" and precisely through this process "causes the destruction of just this thing as a value bearer." By positing an independent world of values and differentiating between them phenomenologically, Scheler arrives at the same dialectical structure of the tragic that already appears in Schelling and Hegel and, in Simmel, is disrobed of its last conceptual vestments. The fact that Scheler's definition of the tragic is rooted in a materialist ethics of value does not diminish its validity, for everything tragic, as Scheler maintains, moves without a doubt "in the sphere of values and the relation of values."[6] This ethics of values, however, produces no new insight into the tragic. Scheler only makes explicit something that is implied in all the earlier definitions by thematizing it in a different context, that is, in the establishment of a phenomenological ethics. Scheler fully demonstrates that he, too, recognized the structure of the tragic in a thought in which he leaves behind the terminology of value ethics and provides a mythological model of all tragic paths. Scheler calls the flight of Icarus tragic because the closer Icarus comes to the sun, the more it melts the wax-fastened wings that bear him upward.[7]

Transition

The history of the philosophy of the tragic is itself not free from the tragic. It resembles the flight of Icarus. The closer thought comes to the general concept, the less that the substantial, the source of thought's uplift, adheres to it. Reaching the height of insight into the structure of the tragic, thought collapses, powerless. At the point where a philosophy, as a philosophy of the tragic, becomes more than the knowledge of the dialectic around which its fundamental concepts assemble, at the point where such a philosophy no longer determines its own tragic outcome, it is no longer philosophy. It therefore appears that philosophy cannot grasp the tragic—or that there is no such thing as *the* tragic.

Walter Benjamin drew the same conclusion. His book *The Origin of the German Mourning Play* is an answer to the crisis that the study of the problem of the tragic ran into at the turn of the century, as seen in Volkelt and Scheler. Although Benjamin relinquishes the general concept of the tragic, the path he takes does not lead back to Aristotle.[1] Benjamin does not replace the philosophy of the tragic with poetics, but rather with the philosophy of the history of tragedy. Benjamin's method is philosophy because he strives to recognize the idea, and not the formal laws of tragic poetry. But he refuses to see the idea of tragedy within a tragic process in itself, as it were, which would be bound neither to a historical situation nor necessarily to the form of tragedy, to art in general. An idea, as defined in Benjamin's epistemological introduction, is neither a universal that would contain the particular nor a concept that would subsume the phenomena, but rather the "objective, virtual arrangement" of the phenomena, their "configuration."[2] Benjamin admittedly arrives at his renunciation of the general concept of the tragic not merely through his method based on the philosophy of history, but also through the object of his study: the mourning play [*Trauerspiel*]. Benjamin's goal is to determine the idea of the mourning play. To this end, he uses the definition of Attic tragedy, which he understands as the counterimage of the Baroque mourning play:

> Tragic poetry is based on the idea of sacrifice. But with respect to its victim—the hero—tragic sacrifice differs from all other kinds, being at once a first and a final sacrifice. It is a final sacrifice in the sense of an atoning sacrifice to gods who are upholding an ancient right; a first sacrifice in the sense of a representative action, in which new aspects of the life of a nation announce themselves. These are different from the ancient, fatal obligations in that they do not refer back to a command from above, but to the life of the hero himself; and they destroy him because they are inadequate for the individual will and benefit only the life of the, as yet unborn, national community. The tragic death has a dual significance: it invalidates the ancient rights of the Olympians, and it offers the hero to the unknown god as the first fruit of a new harvest of humanity.[3]

The role of sacrifice in Benjamin's image of tragedy is joined by two further elements within plot construction and the hero's character that can be seen as dramaturgical correlates of sacrifice. The tragic performance, writes Benjamin, displays in its characters "silent anguish," while for the spectators, "it takes place in the speechless contest of the *agon*."[4] The agonal element already appears in "the hypothetical derivation of the tragic process from the sacrificial race around the *Thymele*," and it returns in the fact that "Attic stage plays took the form of contests."[5] The speechlessness of the hero, which Benjamin had already discussed in the early essay "Fate and Character,"[6] is based, however, on his relation to the community for whom he sacrifices himself:

> The content of the hero's achievements belongs to the community, as does language. Since the community denies this content, it remains unarticulated in the hero. . . . The greater the discrepancy between the tragic word and the situation—which can no longer be called tragic when there is no discrepancy—the more surely the hero has escaped the ancient statutes to which, when they finally overtake him, he throws only the silent shadow of his being, the self, as a sacrifice, while his soul finds refuge in the word of a distant community.[7]

For Benjamin, the idea of tragedy is constituted by the elements of sacrifice, speechlessness, and the agon. By "tragedy" he understands only the tragedy of the Greeks, whose "confrontation with the demonic world-order gives tragic poetry its signature in terms of the philosophy of history."[8]

Nothing would be more foreign to Benjamin's intentions than to want to determine in the configuration of these elements the one element that first produces tragic poetry as such and from which, then, a general concept of the tragic could be extracted. One cannot, however, overlook the fact that Benjamin's analysis of tragic sacrifice closely follows the presentations found in Hölderlin's *Ground for Empedocles* and *Becoming in Passing Away*,[9] in Hegel's discussion of Socrates, and in Hebbel's preface to *Mary Magdalene*.[10] Hegel writes:

> The fate of Socrates is . . . genuinely tragic. . . . The principle of the Greek world could not yet bear the principle of subjective reflection; the latter thus appeared as hostile and destructive. The Athenian people were not only justified but also obliged, according to their laws, to react against it. They therefore perceived the principle of subjective reflection as a crime. This is the position of heroes in world history in general; through them, a new world rises.[11]

Benjamin's concept of sacrifice shares the dialectical structure of these authors' definitions of the tragic. In Benjamin's interpretation, all the following situations must be called tragic: The emancipation from "ancient right" can occur only by revering it once again; the removal of "fatal obligations" demands, in turn, death as its price; the "new aspects of the life of the nation" require for their realization the individual as hero, but must also destroy him, for they are "inadequate for the single will." Benjamin did not want to conclude from the dialectical structure of sacrifice in Greek tragedy that the tragic in general possesses a dialectical essence. Yet neither did he overlook this dialectical structure. It appears, rather, that Benjamin (like Hegel in his early essay "The Spirit of Christianity and Its Fate")[12] posits the genesis of the tragic as identical with the genesis of the dialectic, even if he does not characterize it as such. The above-quoted text on tragic poetry's signature in terms of the philosophy of history continues as follows:

> The tragic is to the demonic what paradox [this is the expression for the dialectical] is to ambiguity. In all the paradoxes of tragedy—in sacrifice,

> which, in complying with ancient statutes, creates new ones; in death, which is an act of atonement and yet only sweeps away the self; in the tragic ending, which grants victory to man, but also to God—ambiguity, the stigma of demons, is in decline.[13]

Whereas paradox saves us from ambiguity in Benjamin, in Hegel, the dialectic saves us from the dualism called forth by the objective law. This difference between Benjamin and Hegel is conspicuous precisely because of the great proximity of their thought. Nor can this difference be adequately explained by the fact that Hegel concentrates mostly on *Antigone* and Benjamin on *Oedipus*. Rather, the fact that Benjamin's tragic hero battles not against a man-made law (as in Hegel), but against a nonhuman, demonic power appears to be historically motivated. Hegel's definitions of the tragic in the texts on natural right and "The Spirit of Christianity" are directed against the remainders of the rationalist Enlightenment. It is precisely in Benjamin, however, that the new Enlightenment, rising up against the irrationalism of the nineteenth and twentieth centuries and its surrender to myth, finds an advocate. After Benjamin, this new Enlightenment is defended in Max Horkheimer's and Theodor W. Adorno's *Dialectic of Enlightenment*, as well as in Bloch's *The Principle of Hope*, whose observations in "Death as the Chisel in Tragedy" take up, not coincidentally, the work of Walter Benjamin.[14]

Although the viewpoint based on the philosophy of history (whose conviction that the tragic is historically conditioned allows it to renounce a general, timeless concept) cannot escape being subjected, for its part, to historical interpretation, it does not forfeit its significance for the understanding of historical forms of tragedy and the mourning play. Nor are its reservations about the philosophy of the tragic, reservations that account for its origination, thereby invalidated. The fact that the philosophy of history's view of the tragic also partakes of the dialectical structure traversing all definitions of the tragic from Schelling to Scheler as their sole constant factor speaks just as little against it. But the necessity of historically limiting the tragic to Attic tragedy is doubtful. Even Benjamin—who not only surrendered the general concept of the tragic, but also believed it was necessary to dismiss German Idealism's entire theory of tragedy as being erroneously based on the concepts of guilt and atonement[15]—comes across the dialectical moment in his interpretation based on the philosophy of history. This dialectical element constitutes the common denominator in the various Idealist and post-Idealist determinations of the tragic and, thereby, the possible basis for its general concept. This is not evident in Benjamin's text primarily because the mourning play is his object of inquiry. When he does go beyond antiquity and the Baroque, he can limit himself to later forms of mourning plays, as found, for example, in the Storm and Stress period or in Schiller's *The Wife of Messina*, without having to consider tragedies such as Schiller's *Demetrius* or Racine's *Phaedra*.

The significance of the dialectical element for the concept of the tragic also arises from the fact that the tragic is already comprehensible when there is no mention of it, but only of tragedy as a concrete artwork: in Aristotle's *Poetics* and among his students. Searching for the plot type that is most appropriate for arousing fear and pity, Aristotle arrives at the claim that the *peripeteia* occurs not as a result of moral depravity, but rather because of the serious offence of a person "of average character or, more preferably, of a person whose character is better rather than worse."[16] Guilt should dialectically emerge from an admittedly only approximate virtuousness, for a misfortune of the truly virtuous hero, according to Aristotle, awakens not fear and pity, but annoyance. In the same manner, another chapter in the *Poetics* grants a special place to the dialectic of hate and love, again grounded in a reflection on the tragic effect: Painful events can be considered extremely dreadful and moving when they occur in amicable relationships, "when, for example, brother kills brother, or a son his father, or a mother her son."[17] Lessing also arrives at the dialectical structure of the tragic through an exploration of tragedy's effect when he asks in "The Hamburg Dramaturgy": "why shouldn't a poet be free to make a tender mother unhappy precisely through her tenderness and, thereby, drive our pity for her to an extreme?"[18] Finally, such formulations even appear in Schiller, who, unlike his contemporaries, remained faithful to Aristotle and attempted to understand tragedy through its effect. In an enumeration of the various forms of the emotionally touching, Schiller writes in his essay "On Tragic Art": "This genre of the emotionally touching is yet surpassed by that genre in which the cause of misfortune is not only not contradictory to morality, but also only possible through morality."[19] And in Schiller's notes for *Demetrius*, one finds the succinct sentence: "If there is to be misfortune, then even the good must cause some damage."[20] The appearance of the dialectic in prephilosophical poetics of tragedy is no less notable than the fact that the dialectic seems to remain unaffected by the essential differences exhibited by Aristotle's, Lessing's, and Schiller's poetic conceptions of the tragic effect.

The dialectical structure of the tragic is thus not reserved for the philosophical perspective; it is familiar to the dramaturgical viewpoint, as well as to that based on the philosophy of history, although almost always in conceptual particularization, so that the dialectic as such is almost never considered to be tragic. The dialectic, however, is valid as a criterion for the definition of the tragic. There is no doubt that among the less significant thinkers who dedicated themselves with a special fondness to the problem of the tragic in the nineteenth century, most were on the right path, even when their theories of the tragic usually cannot be separated from a "pantragic" consideration of the world that is more autobiographical than philosophical. A good example of this tendency is a sentence from Julius Bahnsen's book *The Tragic as the Law of the World and Humor as the Aesthetic Form of the Metaphysical*: "The unconditionally irreconcilable self-division of the innermost core of all being is revealed in the tragic."[21] Another author, Eleutheropulos, defines the tragic as the "negation of life out of inner necessity."[22] Weightier than the one-sidedness of such definitions of the tragic (a one-sidedness that even characterizes influential philosophers and aestheticians) is the overlooking of the dialectical factor, as is evident in J. H. Kirchmann's definition: the tragic is "the demise of the sublime."[23] This definition could be salvaged only if one added: it is the sublimity of the sublime that causes the demise of the sublime, or, man cannot live without the sublime, but precisely through his life, indeed, by realizing the sublime, man must destroy the sublime.

Despite the ubiquity of the dialectical element, a ubiquity that is diminished neither by historical nor methodological borders, one must take into consideration that the aesthetics of German Idealism and later periods persistently refused to put the dialectic at the center of its examinations of the tragic. One of the main reasons for this lies in the fact that the most significant thinkers (Schelling, Hegel, Hölderlin, as well as Solger and Schopenhauer) were not primarily interested in defining the tragic. Rather, they ran across a phenomenon within their own philosophies that they called the tragic, although it was only *one* tragic phenomenon: the crystallization of the tragic in their thought. The timidity in the face of a dialectical determination of the tragic also stems from the fact that it is in no way sufficient, that it refuses to give way to reversibility. If the tragic were the demise of the sublime, then it would always be tragic when something sublime meets its end. But because not every form of dialectics is tragic, the tragic must be recognized as a particular form of dialectics within a particular space, especially by differentiating it from its counterconcepts, which are also dialectically structured: the comical, irony, and humor.[24] This task remains reserved for a further study. In a more decisive fashion, the above-mentioned timidity may be motivated by the fact that it is not considered permissible to reduce a phenomenon such as the tragic to the formal-logical concept of the dialectic, particularly when the tragic is responsible for the highest level of poetry and is always understood in connection with the meaning of being. This meaning, however, must be determined always anew in the analysis of individual tragedies, while the definitions of the tragic since Schelling are always guided by the particular meaning of the philosopher, by his metaphysical design. In this respect, the philosophy of the tragic is in accord with tragic poetry: Instead of speaking of Schopenhauer's definition of the tragic, it would be more correct to speak of the tragic in Schopenhauer, of a Schopenhauerian form of the tragic—just as one speaks of a Shakespearean form of the tragic.

One can draw no other consequence from this than the one drawn from the crisis to which the dialectical conception of the tragic in the post-Idealist era led: There is no such thing as *the* tragic, at least not as an essence. Rather, the tragic is a mode, a particular manner of destruction that is threatening or already completed: the dialectical manner. There is only *one* tragic downfall: the one that results from the unity of opposites, from the sudden change into one's opposite, from self-division. But it is also the case that only the demise of something that should not meet its demise, whose removal does not allow the wound to heal, is tragic. The tragic contradiction may not be sublated in a superordinate sphere, whether immanent or transcendent. If this is the case, then either the object of destruction was something trivial, which as such eludes the tragic and offers itself to the comic, or the tragic is already vanquished in humor, covered up in irony, or surmounted in faith. Kierkegaard, more than any other, had considered this; a valid theory of the tragic and its counterconcepts can be extracted from his works, particularly from *Stages on Life's Way* and *Concluding Unscientific Postscript.*

The following section can address only a much smaller topic. Using eight tragedies as examples, it attempts to strengthen the thesis of the tragic's dialectical structure, of the tragic as a dialectical modality. To strengthen a thesis is not to prove it, but to test it. The gaze that falls upon these tragedies searches for their dialectical construction. The sign that this view is correct lies not in finding this construction, but in it deepening one's understanding of the tragedies. Admittedly, the eight examinations are not interpretations, but merely analyses, and, to be precise, analyses of the tragic in these pieces, often only the tragic process undergone by a single figure. Nor do they pose questions that go above and beyond the text itself. The analyses neither presuppose a concept of the tragic determined by content (as in Hegel's concept based on the conflict between two representatives of right), nor do they inquire into a text's explicit "content": into the poet's intention or the meaning of the play.

Because the concept of the tragic disastrously rises out of the concrete situation of philosophical problems into the heights of abstraction, it must sink down into the most concrete element of tragedies if it is to be saved. This most concrete element is the plot. Plot, of course, is looked down upon in reflections on the tragic. Yet plot is the most important constituent of drama, which, not accidentally, owes its name to the Greek word for the plot's action. The validity of the dialectical conception of the tragic will therefore be recognizable if the most inconspicuous plot elements can still be successfully seen in their relation to the tragic construction and the work then be seen as a seamless whole.

The eight tragedies are intended only to be examples. The selection of texts took place according to various perspectives. They should be representative for the four great epochs of tragic poetry: the age of Greek tragedians; the Baroque era in Spain, England, and Germany; French classicism; and the age of Goethe. In some cases, possible connections (e.g., between Calderon and Sophocles) were taken into consideration, as were prejudices (as in the case in Shakespeare and Calderon) and even tragic acuteness: hence the choice of Kleist's first work and Schiller's last one.

PART II

Analyses of the Tragic

ACHILLES:
Thus spake the eagle, when he saw the feathers
On the arrow that pierced him:
Thus we are slain by none other
Than our own wings.

—Aeschylus

§ 13 *Oedipus Rex*

The tragic weaves its way through the plot fabric of *Oedipus Rex* as through no other work. At every point in the hero's fate, he is met with the unity of salvation and annihilation, a fundamental trait of everything tragic. It is not annihilation that is tragic, but the fact that salvation becomes annihilation; the tragic does not take place in the hero's downfall, but rather in the fact that man meets his demise along the very path he took up to escape this demise. Such is the tragic hero's fundamental experience; it is confirmed with each of his steps and, at best, only ultimately gives way to another experience: that the road to ruin ends in salvation and redemption.

Unlike in Aeschylus, the gods no longer appear as figures in Sophocles' dramas. But they do participate in the events. The hero is neither fully granted nor fully denied freedom. Therefore Oedipus says: "I'll do everything. Yet it is God/Who brings us salvation or ruin."[1] That the gods bestow something dreadful on humanity is, however, not tragic. Rather, it is tragic when the dreadful occurs through man's own doing. The fact that man implores the god (who puts himself into words as the oracle) to intervene in his doings is, therefore, no less important for this tragedy than the silent, divine power over the events.

The oracle speaks three times in the course of *Oedipus Rex*: first to Laios, then to his son, and finally to Creon, who consults the oracle on Oedipus's behalf. Three times the oracle turns divine knowledge into human knowledge, three times it thereby guides human action and allows the characters to carry out what has been imposed upon them. At these three points, the tragic tightens itself into knots within the plot fabric; only through these three points is the tragic to be resolved. Admittedly, these moments are not the main ones in Sophocles' play. His "tragic analysis" first begins with the last oracle.[2] By fulfilling the oracle's demand, the "tragic analysis" invokes the first two oracles; the meaning of Oedipus's cry: "O, o, the whole thing is coming out clearly!"[3] summarizes all three oracles and forms his fate from them.

I

Laios's oracle, the origin of the entire action, is transmitted in several versions.[4] According to Aeschylus, Laios is told that Thebes would survive only if he remained childless. In order to have descendants, he must renounce having descendants; the heir, who otherwise saves the lineage from demise, would in this case bring about its demise. The tragic dialectic of salvation and annihilation is thus already present at the very beginning. It is common to both Sophocles' and Euripides' versions that the king knows the prediction of his son murdering him. The one he fathers shall destroy him; the one he has given life shall take his. Even before his birth, Oedipus embodies the tragic unity of creation and annihilation that is related to the other tragic unity traversing the entire work: salvation and annihilation. In Euripides, the oracle takes the form of an admonishing ban. Overcome by drunkenness and desire, Laios fathers a child and becomes guilty through no fault of his own. To save himself, he decides to kill his son and thus repeats the tragic fate of the oracle in reverse: he takes the life of one to whom he first gave life. Because the oracle does not appear as a warning in Sophocles, his tragic fate is further heightened. Without previously being forbidden to produce a son, Laios learns that he will one day be killed by him. Unlike a warning, this knowledge no longer admits the possibility of being saved. There is no course of action that would be appropriate for him. The knowledge suggests that he should murder his son while simultaneously proving the idea to be futile: The knowledge is salvation and annihilation in one. Whether Laios believes the oracle or not (Jocasta will later choose to be skeptical), it does not change his situation: Belief and doubt alike should hinder him in resolving to kill his son. However, instead of accepting the tragic rift that he cannot do what he must do (and the reason for not doing it is not the same for having to do it), Laios acts as if he knew that his son might kill him, and not as if he knows that his son will kill him. To escape the tragic, he uses the most nontragic means imaginable: inconsistency.[5] Yet inconsistency is not his salvation, but his downfall. When Laios takes the road to Delphi to find out from the oracle (according to Euripides) if his son is really dead—his uncertainty is the consequence of his inconsistency—he actually goes to meet his son and is killed by him at the crossroads.

2

The oracle speaks a second time to the young Oedipus, who has been abandoned by his parents in the ravines of Cithaeron, saved by a shepherd, and raised by Polybos, the king of Corinth, as an adopted son. When a drunk man at a banquet claims that Oedipus is not Polybos's son and that Polybos is concealing the truth, Oedipus leaves for Delphi. Yet instead of telling him who his parents are, the oracle announces something horrifying, for the sake of which it would be necessary for Oedipus to know who his parents are: He is to be his father's murderer and his mother's spouse. Consulting the oracle thus turns salvation into annihilation: Instead of putting an end to his ignorance of his true parents, it turns this ignorance into the cause of the future dreadful events. The oracle puts Oedipus in a position that at first appears to be similar to Laios's in Sophocles. Here it is also the case that one is not warned against what could happen, but rather learns in advance what will happen. Oedipus's tragic situation, however, is intensified not only by the oracle's message being expanded and appearing as God's command, so that he, fearing God, must want what he cannot possibly want, but also by the fact that a stoic attitude is no longer possible for him. While Laios fled from his murderer, Oedipus flees from becoming a murderer himself. Unlike his father, Oedipus is forced to act, for he must prevent his own actions. He therefore decides not to return to Corinth and heads for Thebes. But the flight from his supposed parents leads him to his true father. For the first time in the Oedipus plot, a gaping hole opens up between being and appearance,[6] which offers the tragic dialectic a new field of play: salvation within the realm of appearances proves itself in reality to be destruction. Father and son thus stand face to face at the crossroads without recognizing one another. The father wants to consult the oracle about his son; the son has already consulted it about his father. Yet instead of learning who his father is, Oedipus only learns what he now flees from, so as to fulfill the oracle through the very act of fleeing.

3

To free Thebes from the plague, Creon consults the Delphic oracle on Oedipus's behalf, and the oracle speaks a third time. It answers by demanding that Laios's murder be avenged. Unlike the first two oracles, this demand no longer presages something horrifying, but promises salvation by expiating a horror that has already occurred. The Thebans turn to Oedipus, for he has already saved them from the Sphinx and thus became their king. Once again he seems to be given to them as a savior. Fearing that Laios's murderers also want to kill him, Oedipus thinks that he can save himself by arresting them. Yet as soon as the investigation begins and Tiresias calls the king "a stain in our land,"[7] Oedipus intuits that the promised salvation holds the seed of his destruction. The hope of finding Laios's murderer meets, in contrapuntal fashion, the dread of recognizing himself as the murderer. In the course of the investigation, everything that appears to protect the king from the salvation that will destroy him turns, for its part, into his destruction. To the shame of the seer Tiresias, Jocasta tells the story of Laios's oracle and of his murder, not by his son's hand, but by thieves at the crossroads. Instead of reassuring Oedipus, Jocasta awakens in him the first presentiment of his guilt. The messenger's revelation has the same effect: He reports that Oedipus is not Polybos's son and, therefore, need not fear Corinth, for the oracle cannot prove to be true there. It is now almost certain for Oedipus that the oracle has proven itself to be true. Oedipus places his last hopes in the shepherd, for he described the murderers as robbers. And yet it is the shepherd himself who uncovers the dreadful truth. In the shepherd's confession, which Oedipus must tear from him, the tragic unity of salvation and annihilation returns: In order to save his own life, Laios had condemned his son to death; the shepherd wanted to spare the son, but "saved him for the gravest ignominy."[8] The murderer that Oedipus seeks is himself. The savior of

Thebes proves himself to be simultaneously its destroyer. Oedipus is not *also* a destroyer, but rather precisely a destroyer as a savior, for the plague is the gods' punishment for the reward he received for his saving action: the incestuous marriage with Queen Jocasta. The acumen that showed him "Man" in the riddle of the Sphinx and thereby saved Thebes did not allow him to recognize the man that he himself is and, thus, led him to his ruin. The duel between Oedipus and Tiresias, between the one who sees, yet is blind, and the blind seer, ends with Oedipus's self-blinding. The eyesight that concealed from him what he should have seen and what the blind Tiresias saw shall no longer show him what he, now too late, continually ought to see.

In retrospect, the first two oracles prove themselves to be prefigurations of the decisive third oracle, which Sophocles places in the middle of his tragedy. Both Laios and the young Oedipus take up the tragic path between Thebes and Delphi, between human blindness and divine revelation. Oedipus follows this road to avoid becoming a murderer, Laios to avoid being murdered. And yet the road leads the one to death and the other to murder. As the path of knowledge in *Oedipus Rex*, the road between Thebes and Delphi is, so to speak, turned inward. Prehistory's epic wandering is condensed in this tragedy into a dramatic reconnaissance mission. Disaster awaits the king not as a stranger at the edge of the road, but at the destination of his own knowledge. In the three destinies that at the same time constitute a single destiny, the oracles mark a tragic intensification in which opposed entities become more and more tightly bound together and duality is more and more unsparingly driven to unity: Laios flees his murderer along the path that leads him to his murderer—the young Oedipus tries to escape his prophesized act of murder only to commit it while fleeing—King Oedipus searches for Laios's murderers, whom he fears will be his own murderers, and finds himself.

§ 14 *Life Is a Dream*

I

Even before his birth, the life of the Polish prince Sigismund stands under the sign of disaster—just like the life of the Theban king's son. Calderon's piece is called a Christian Oedipus play with good reason. The weakening of prophecy, however, testifies to the changes that the Oedipus motif undergoes in the Catholic Baroque. The death of the mother replaces incest. Even if Sigismund causes her death through his birth, it remains a natural occurrence, while Oedipus's incestuous marriage takes place as his own action, even if he doesn't know its true nature. And parricide gives way to a militarylike subjugation that, like the death of the mother, shifts things into a more general context and goes beyond individual fate: Following upon nature, this context is now history. Although the insight that lends the play its title ultimately rescues the events from the tragic, its foundation is no less bound up in the tragic than *Oedipus Rex.* And instead of weakening Greek tragedy, the changes demanded by the Christian faith initially call forth only new tragic moments. The first of these new tragic factors already occurs with the prophecy of disaster. In *Life Is a Dream*, prophecy no longer takes place in the universally valid, institutional form of the oracle, but rather makes use of two contradictory sources: the dream and science. It thus touches upon a division in man's nature that questions his wholeness. On the one hand, the pregnant queen sees in a dream a humanlike monster that kills her. On the other, the king's astrological knowledge (the source of his greatest fame and, as it were, his rule over the age) reveals to him how his son will one day affront him. Because prophecy in

Calderon, as in Shakespeare's *Macbeth*, no longer bears the authority of the oracle, it turns to deception. If prophecy's first part comes true on its own, man lends credence to the second part and acts accordingly. This action, however, is what first tragically draws him into guilt. Thus, Macbeth interprets his being named Thane of Cawdor (for which his battle merits provide reason enough) as a sign of the witches speaking the truth and views regicide as fulfilling the task that fate posed to him. Thus, the queen's death while giving birth to her child appears to Basilio as proof of the prophecy's accuracy, and he now believes in its second half. The irony of fate in Shakespeare lies in Macbeth's taking the reward for his virtue as the guarantee for the future success of his vice; the irony of fate in Calderon consists in the king trusting his science because the unconscious seems to have spoken the truth. In addition to the tragic element that this irony produces in its victim, there is a second tragic factor that no longer lies in knowledge's dependence on the unconscious, but in science itself. The king's famous ability to read the future in the stars, after it has established his greatness, turns into his destruction: "For the unfortunate ones,/Merit itself becomes a knife;/And he who harms himself through knowledge/Is his own murderer."[1]

2

The powers that allow Basilio and Laios to see into the future do not permit either of them to avoid what has been seen. If they believe it, they must accept it; if they doubt it, they have nothing to fear and, thus, nothing to undertake. But if they act, they do so out of inconsistency. Admittedly, the belief in prophecy imposes itself less on Basilio than on Laios. Whereas the oracle speaks in the name of Apollo, the double prophecy of the Polish king is not strengthened by his Christian faith, but placed in doubt. Basilio must ask himself whether he sins against his God when he trusts the dream and the stars and thereby puts superstition and science before God. Catholicism believes in free will; Sigismund's actions cannot therefore be predetermined. But even the thought of his son's freedom to act as he sees fit must remind Basilio of the disaster that the stars prophesized through his son's hands. Like Laios, Basilio attempts to avert what has been predicted: He takes it merely as a danger, and not as the future fact that it is. The doubt incited by his faith allows him to be more careful in his attempt to fend off the prophecy than Laios, who only in Euripides begins to doubt whether the measures he takes are successful, but not whether they are justified. Whereas the Theban king destines his son for a supposedly certain death by having him abandoned in the ravines of Cithaeron, Basilio orders his newborn son to be locked in a tower. Whereas Laios submits to the delusion that he is protecting himself from his future murderer by having him preemptively murdered, Basilio imagines that he can keep his son alive, but prevent him from performing the deed that has been foretold. Even this, however, proves itself to be a deception whose victim is the one who hoped to be saved by it. The victim's moment arrives when Basilio, plagued by doubts about the correctness of his former measures against his son, puts the now adult son to the test. Put to sleep by a drink, the son is led into the palace and awakens there as its ruler. Through this test, which itself bears a tragic element, Calderon's play completely frees itself from antiquity and realizes a central idea of the Baroque: the world as theater. The world as theater exists here, though, without allegorical figures (as is also the case in the *auto sacramental*[2] version of the same play), but rather as a parable, that is, with individuals as dramatis personae.[3] One after the other, representatives of the court and the royal family appear before the regally clothed prince to see if the stars are right in destining him to be a tyrant. His behavior seems to concede the prophecy's truth. Yet in every detail of his tyrannical manner, it becomes clear that he speaks and acts in this way not because it is his natural disposition, but because in the tower he has become such a man. The monster that demonstrates the truth of the queen's dream is not the creature of fate, but rather the creature of the one who strove to avert it, the king himself. His attempt to fend off the prophecy gave rise to what his efforts should have prevented. Not only the prince's banishment, but also the test that is intended to compensate for this banishment converts salvation into destruction. The test Sigismund undergoes unexpectedly makes him the tester. Cut off from every sense of possibility in the tower's imprisonment, he now strives to realize the impossible. Sigismund, therefore, condemns a courtier to death and threatens Rosaura with rape: "To conquer the impossible/Is my desire; today one was forced to leap from the balcony/Despite his insistence that such things cannot happen here./Now, to see my own potency, I would like/To grant your chaste honor such a leap."[4] To no avail, Rosaura proves herself to be the only one who sees that the cause of Sigismund's behavior does not lie in his natural disposition, but in the life imposed upon him by his father: "Could it prove to be otherwise/For one who is human only in name?/For one who grew up with wild animals,/Proud and high-spirited, barbaric, impudent, inhuman, and cruel?"[5] Like Basilio's attempt to fend off the prophecy, Rosaura's insight threatens to become ruinous within a tragic dialectic that also returns in Kleist's *The Schroffenstein Family*. Sigismund replies to her: "And yet if I am what your lips call me,/Then you, too, should, by God!, know me completely." The villain is or behaves as the handiwork of the one who considers or knows him to be a villain. The test culminates in the second appearance of the king. Sigismund hurls a string of words at the king that promise the prophecy's fulfillment (Basilio's white hair will become the rug for Sigismund's feet), but also show that the one who sought to thwart the prophecy will bear the guilt: "Perhaps—it can happen—/I will see your hair at my feet;/For I must indeed punish you,/Because you raised me as a slave without rights."[6] Admittedly, the king is initially spared the knowledge that both things turn against him: his attempt to fend off the prophecy as well as his testing of the need to fend it off in the first place. Deluded that he can undo what has been done, the king once again has the prince put to sleep and brought into the isolation of the tower.

3

The Christian sphere changes antiquity's tragic process of fate into the tragic process of individuality and consciousness. The Greek hero unknowingly commits the terrible deed by trying to avoid it. Before his redemption, the Catholic drama's hero is a victim of his attempt to use knowledge and thought to replace a threatening reality with another that he himself has created. The three acts of Calderon's play delineate this difference (whereby Oedipus no longer corresponds to Sigismund, but to Basilio) with ever greater clarity. To the tragic aspect of prophecy the first act adds the tragic aspect of knowledge, a knowledge that turns the king into "his own murderer." No longer having anything in common with antiquity, the second act forms the tragic process of the endeavor to influence the life of another through an invented mode for fending off prophecy, rather than through sympathetic help. The attempt to render Sigismund harmless first makes him harmful, because Basilio overlooks the fact that attempting to avert prophecy is no mere negative action: It not only thwarts, but also brings about. Basilio does not leave his son to his natural disposition and then see if he truly is destined to be a tyrant. Rather, Basilio calls forth the prophesized disposition instead of suppressing it. Finally, the tragic outcome of the test appears in the third act, before the play leaves the space of the tragic, as is the case in all Christian drama. In his arrogant thinking, Basilio gives in to the delusion that he can experiment with reality and thereby create one that would remain without consequences. Yet this attempt to transform into a dream the life that Sigismund briefly lived as a king fails. As soon as the king's intention of destining the crown not for his son, but for his sister's children is made known, rebellious factions assemble against him. The rebels do not see the prince's rule as the prince himself sees it—as a dream—and therefore choose him as their leader. Basilio thinks he owes the possibility of avoiding his son's rule to the prophecy of the dream, yet it is this that first makes his son ruler. Sigismund declares himself willing to lead the revolt only because he sees in the dream—the one that his father made of his kingship during the reality of the test—the prophetic sign of his destiny as king. The battle against Basilio leads the rebels to victory. Only now, after an attempt to fend off the prophecy (through Sigismund's banishment) and a further attempt to make good on this fending off (in case it was unfounded), is the prophecy fulfilled for the king: he kneels, conquered, at the feet of his son. With great precision, he formulates the dialectic of his tragic fate, a dialectic that he shares with Oedipus: "Fate's rule is irresistible,/ And it is often dangerous to foresee fate./Human limitations cannot protect themselves;/For by fearfully protecting, one lures wicked events. /Cruel precept! Hard fate! Terrible injury!/To flee danger first leads to danger./What should protect me becomes my disaster;/I, I myself caused my kingdom's ruin."[7] The exemplary death of the servant Clarion, who is fatally wounded when, cowardly, he hides and imagines himself safe, prompts Basilio to reiterate this insight: "To spare my kingdom from rebellion and ruin/I entrusted it to the hand that I sought to tear it away from."[8] At this point, where Calderon's piece could end as tragedy, the downfall to which salvation seems to lead changes, for its part, into its opposite, and becomes salvation. The road to ruin, which the road to salvation proved itself to be, ultimately reveals itself as the road to salvation, but now no longer through a turn of fate, but rather through the insight of man himself. And as in all great literature that does not end in the tragic, the way out of the tragic is the inversion of the road that leads into it. For Basilio, the test that began as salvation and turned into disaster ultimately swings back to salvation. In its first manifestation, the dream shows Sigismund before his birth as a monster and thereby grounds the tragic events. In its second manifestation, in the king's test, the dream enables Sigismund truly to become ruler, rather than allowing him forget his rule as a dream. The dream ultimately proves itself to be Sigismund's mentor and, thus, the king's savior. Sigismund does not forget the test as a dream, but rather learns that all of life is a dream. Defying the prophecy of the stars, he decides that in life (which is, henceforth, considered only to be a dream) he will be different than he was in the dream he took for life.

§ 15 *Othello*

I

Shakespeare's literary model is an Italian novella, *The Moor of Venice*. The title refers to one of the antagonistic elements that determine the tragic events. Othello is a Moor and a Venetian. As a Venetian, he is to have command of the fleet; as a Moor, he is not allowed to wed a Venetian. The city's inhabitants consider the warrior to be their equal, but the lover to be a black animal. In a turbulent counterpoint, the first act illustrates this division of Othello: In the nocturnal streets of Venice, two sides search for him. The father whose daughter he stole pursues him to deliver him over to the courts, while the doge looks for Othello to entrust him with the command of the fleet. It is particularly characteristic of *Othello* that the conflict is not fought out in the doge's palace, but only later within Othello himself. Corneille's heroes are also painfully aware that as lovers and warriors they cannot be one and the same person. Their tragic conflict—"the crossing of two necessities"—is, however, capricious in its origin and external to them.[1] Admittedly, Corneille's heroes can neither follow their inclination and their duty simultaneously nor disregard one of them. But they are not attacked in their inner being: Neither as lover nor as warrior are they called into question. Othello, on the contrary, immediately succeeds in obtaining from the doge both the honorable appointment as fleet commander and the approval of his marriage. But in his heart, he takes away from this success his own self-doubt. Man often views himself through the eyes of another, and although Othello knows himself to be of royal lineage, in Cyprus, he will never be able to forget how he saw himself in the Venetian mirror. Although Desdemona gave Othello proof of her love, Othello's self-confidence is undermined by Desdemona's father's not only disapproving of this love, but also disbelieving it—and therefore accusing Othello of magic. Upon this ground of shaken belief in oneself, Iago brings jealousy into bloom.

2

Unlike other passions, jealousy bears within itself the possibility of the tragic. Even before colliding with another power, the one seized by jealousy is branded a tragic hero. The essence of jealousy lies in the dialectic, which admittedly also allows it to turn into the comical. Jealousy is love that destroys by wanting to preserve. Othello's parting kiss is accompanied by the words: "O balmy breath, that dost almost persuade / Justice to break her sword. One more, one more! / Be thus when thou art dead, and I will kill thee / And love thee after."[2]

3

Othello is a victim of Iago's revenge. Iago is an ironist; his method is Socratic. Therefore, Iago's image of himself trickling poison into Othello's ear is not entirely accurate. Just as Socrates finds his students guilty of ignorance, Iago finds Othello guilty of jealousy. His plan is characterized by an ironic joy in finding and imparting opposites, in turning good into evil. "So will I turn her virtue into pitch; / And out of her own goodness make the net / That shall enmesh them all," Iago says of Desdemona, who, by helping the dismissed Cassio, supposedly betrays her adulterous love for him.[3] But the scene in which Iago induces the birth of Othello's jealousy (to use the Socratic metaphor) is probably the most perfect realization of the irony of action, which is far more rare than the irony of observation. Iago, a second Socrates, acts in "absolute negativity" in relation to Othello.[4] What Iago achieves, he always achieves through its opposite. His questions are answers, his answers questions; his "yes" conceals a "no," his "no" a "yes." Othello's disquiet is the work of Iago's attempts to quiet him; Othello's doubt is the effect of Iago's attempts to convince him. Iago names the destination to which he wants to lead Othello under the pretense of warning him against going there. Othello thus arrives there by his own doing, just as he also first mentioned Cassio's name. Iago's irony thereby heightens the tragic in Othello. Not only does Othello destroy by wanting to preserve, but he also destroys no longer as a victim of Iago, but as a victim of himself. The divine irony that stood opposite the tragic hero in antiquity is replaced in the Baroque by the irony of the villain.

4

"Give me the ocular proof," Othello exclaims as his jealousy takes possession of him.[5] This tormenting demand for proof belongs to the dialectic of doubt, which has its tragic side. The doubt about a wife's fidelity—born out of the fear of her infidelity—seeks its proof not in fidelity, but in infidelity. Othello's doubts can be put to rest only by the evidence that proves him right, not by the evidence that proves him a liar. And this is his only wish. What Othello fears the most is, then, precisely what he longs for the most. Iago knows that the least of evidence will be sufficient enough for the jealous one. What he offers Othello is the handkerchief that Othello once gave to Desdemona as a present and is now in Cassio's hands. Like the letter in Schiller's *Don Carlos*, the handkerchief takes on a pernicious power over Othello, a power that is tragic because he hands himself over to this power. The possibility of doubting the proof is foreign to Othello. This is the case not only because he yearns to quench the doubts that plague him like thirst, but also because he seeks refuge from the man he does not trust (for Iago can don any role) in the object he does trust (for he believes the handkerchief is capable of doing no harm). Precisely because the object cannot tell its own lies, it is difficult to see through its lies. For Othello, the fact that Desdemona gives away the handkerchief, which he then sees in Cassio's possession, counts as proof of his wife's infidelity. Yet Desdemona's giving of the handkerchief is her gesture of love for Othello, for she does so to soothe his headache. When Othello turns it down, Emilia takes it and gives it to Iago, who brings it into Cassio's room. The headache that Othello claims to suffer from is only the alias for his passion. The handkerchief thus becomes an emblem for an element in Desdemona's tragic fate. With the handkerchief she unknowingly sets ablaze what she sought to extinguish: Othello's jealousy.

5

Desdemona is accompanied to Cyprus by her father's curse: "Look to her, Moor, if thou hast eyes to see: / She has deceived her father, and may thee."[6] This argument has its place in Iago's plan. Because Othello is not naturally distrustful, Iago must make Othello believe that Desdemona could deceive him, and therefore reminds him of the deception to which he owes her love for him. Othello is now finally ready to disregard Desdemona's affirmations and to trust only the handkerchief. What had united Othello and Desdemona in front of all of Venice divides them in his soul. Their marriage falls apart on the very thing that had established it. What Desdemona did for Othello's sake now proves only that she is capable of doing it again, now in an act of unfaithfulness to Othello. The proof of her love turns into the proof of her infidelity. The ironist's dialectical method thereby transforms man into the opposite of himself. The loving wife appears as the adulteress; the lover becomes the murderer of the one he loves.

§ 16 *Leo Armenius*

Gryphius's first dramatic work simultaneously counts as the first tragedy of German literature. For a long time it remained perhaps the only one. In *Catharine of Georgia*, Gryphius already had moved from tragedy to the mourning play and from then on remained faithful to this latter genre when addressing a serious subject matter.[1] As for Calderon, the all-uniting force of the Christian message of salvation eliminates the tragic rupture for Gryphius. *Leo Armenius*, therefore, does not remain within the parameters of antiquity, although its central idea is purely tragic and determined by the study of the ancients. Rather, it integrates the Christian religion itself into the tragic field of tension. Instead of turning the believer into a martyr whose faith relieves his tragic fate, the Christian religion becomes his tragic lot. Christianity does not provide the believer with his desired and promised salvation, but with a downfall that the crucifix (the place of his demise) does not transfigure, but rather contrapuntally intensifies within the tragic process he undergoes.[2]

I

The past binds Leo Armenius, the emperor of Constantinople, and Michael Balbus, his highest-ranking captain, who has conspired against him. Years ago as a commander in the battle with the Bulgarians, Leo broke from his emperor and named himself the new emperor with the help of his friend. Their later enmity, which forms the basis of the events unfolding before and during Christmas 820, occurs in a twilight that disallows the separation of good from evil and shows two mutually exclusive tragic fates neither of which can be understood as merely feigned or pretended. If Leo Armenius is a tyrant whose death is necessary for the country's salvation, then Michael Balbus's tragic fate consists in the fact that the one he helped to become emperor so as to save Byzantium has become Byzantium's destroyer. If Leo is not a tyrant, then Balbus's tragic lot lies in the fact that he is being threatened with death by the one he himself helped come to power. And the principle guiding the desire to remove Leo Armenius from the throne is, in both cases, the same principle that first put him on the throne: the principle of rebellion and self-appointment.

2

As soon as the conspiracy becomes known, Exabolius advises the king to have Michael Balbus killed. Leo fears, however, that murdering the powerful captain without first judging him could stir up the populace and the ensuing hostility could turn against him. Under the delusion of avoiding his own death, Leo takes the first step toward his own downfall, just as Michael Balbus brings about his own condemnation. Running into a disgruntled Exabolius, whom he considers to be a friend, Balbus thinks that he, too, is disgruntled about the emperor and therefore reveals his intention of killing Leo. At the close of the first act, the chorus of courtiers uses the dialectic's tripartite progression to formulate the tragic process suffered by a man whose own words can turn against him. The closing lines of the three parts, denoted as "Position," "Opposition," and "Addition," read: "The life of man rests upon his tongue"; "The death of man rests upon the tongue of every man"; "Hold your life, o man, and your death always on your tongue!"[3]

3

Leo takes the second step toward his own death when he postpones the execution of the condemned Balbus in order not to desecrate the celebration of Jesus' birth with murder. The emperor is forced to take this measure by the empress, who, under the delusion of preventing an infringement of Christianity, causes Leo's death. The Christian faith does not appear here as the highest power, one that would be entrusted with leading the hero entangled in the world's antagonisms to triumph in the moment of his demise. The glory of martyrdom illuminates neither the emperor nor the empress, both of whom fall victim to their own religion. Faith has so little power over the events and is so enmeshed in the world that it has to give itself over to protecting the murderers of the one who remained faithful. The night of Christ's birth, which Leo did not want to defile through murder, offers the conspirators the opportunity to kill him. The desecration that the emperor strove to avoid is thus carried out on him. Disguised as priests, Balbus's accomplices steal into the church where Leo is attending service and kill him with daggers that were concealed in candles—emblems of the tragic, in which the darkness of death comes from the light of faith.

4

The fact that Balbus contacts his accomplices from prison and gets them to commit the murder on Christmas is, in tragic fashion, the emperor's own work. Startled by a ghost who predicts in a dream that Michael will kill him, Leo rushes to the prison to ease his mind through the sight of the bound conspirator. He sees him, however, in royal purple, with the guard obedient at his feet. Because Leo thereby knows that Michael has allies both in the palace and in the city, it is not difficult for Michael to convince the conspirators of the danger that now threatens them. To avert this danger, they decide to kill the emperor, but learn, for their part, what is tragic in prophecy, as the final chorus attests: "Those whom the heavens warn through signs, / Can scarcely escape, indeed, cannot escape; / And one sees many, who, by trying to flee death, / Move toward death."[4] The inseparability of good and evil in this world corresponds to the cynical prediction of the spirit who, in response to a conspirator's request for advice before the emperor's murder, answers: "What Leo now bears will come to you."[5] The magician's interpretation is: "What the spirit explains to us / Appears to have two meanings. Your reward will be / What Leo bears. Indeed! What does he bear? The crown and death! / I fear that one will crush you in the same need."[6] The prophecy refers to more than the tragedy's conclusion and the conspirators' triumph: As the reward for helping to dispose of Leo, one of the conspirators is promised Leo's own fate.

5

After the murder of the emperor, the play becomes the tragedy of the empress. She herself is to blame for her husband's death and for what she believes to be her own impending death. In a phrase familiar to the king in *Life is a Dream*, she says: "It is quite something: The cruelest man on earth / Is the one who through his empathy must become his own executioner."[7] Her tragic fate, however, has not yet been fulfilled. Leo's murderer, whose life she saved, denies her the death that she now requests as her form of life. The empress's life is spared out of a gratitude that is cruelty. She thus leaves the stage not as one about to die, but with words of madness that resemble a parody of what Gryphius denied her: the martyr's triumphant vision. Viewing the corpse and surrounded by conspirators, she speaks the words: "O unexpected delight! O greeting that refreshes the soul! / Welcome, worthy Prince! Lord of our senses! / Companions! Mourn no more! He lives."[8]

Just as *Leo Armenius* stands in bold opposition to Gryphius's later martyr dramas, it also as a tragedy deepens the Baroque motif of transience into its own tragic foundation. Rising and falling are not understood merely in their rapid oscillation, but also in their dialectical identity. This is most clearly the case in the verses in which the metaphoric succeeds in grasping the essence of the tragic: "We rise as smoke that disappears in the air, / We rise after the fall, and he who finds lofty heights, / Finds what can topple him."[9]

§ 17 *Phaedra*

I

Forbidden, concealed, unfulfilled—thus is Phaedra's love for Hippolytus. What passion demands of her, Phaedra forbids herself out of faithfulness to Theseus. Instead of uniting Phaedra with her beloved, love divides her within herself. If she could renounce her love or fidelity, the inner conflict would be resolved and the tragic would be eliminated through compromise. Because she can do neither, because the possibility of both lies within her and yet not within her power, she is a tragic heroine. Nonetheless, this tragic dilemma in Racine proves itself to be merely the external face of a deeper inner conflict, one that prevails not between love and duty, but within the heart of love alone.[1] Phaedra loves Hippolytus not only despite his being the son of her husband, but also because he is his son. What stands in the way of her love for him is at the same time her love's motivation. Phaedra loves in Hippolytus the Theseus who once came to Crete and who no longer existed after he wed her: "Yes, Prince, I languish and I long for Theseus./I love him, but not as the Shades know him:/The inconstant lover of so many loves,/Who now would ravish even Pluto's bride!/But faithful, proud, even to a slight disdain;/Young, charming, drawing all hearts after him,/As gods are painted. Or as I see you now."[2] This deception, which maintains the semblance of marital fidelity even in the midst of declaring love for another, is possible only because faithfulness and unfaithfulness are entwined in Phaedra's heart. Her love for the former Theseus draws her to his son—incest, as far as the word is meaningful here, is for Phaedra the sign of an overpowering bond to an image that reality cannot satisfy. Phaedra's love for the pure image of Theseus not only awakens her love for Hippolytus, but also simultaneously prevents this love from being fulfilled. If Hippolytus were to yield to Phaedra, he would lose precisely what Phaedra loves in him. In a tragic manner, her love falters not first on its opponent—duty—but on itself, on the fact that it is for the one who is innocent and pure. Phaedra could possess this love only in sin, and only in sin could Phaedra destroy it. For Phaedra's love, there is not only no path leading to its fulfillment, but also no path that she could take to escape it. Every road she takes leads back to Hippolytus and deepens her love for him without bringing it closer to fulfillment. The prayers and sacrifices she offers to Venus to be freed from her love become, against her will, gifts for the beloved, in whom she recognizes her god: "In vain my hand burnt incense at Her shrine:/ When my mouth invoked the goddess' name, my heart adored/Hippolytus; and, always seeing him,/Continually, even at the foot/Of altars that I made for Her,/I worshipped the god whose name I dared not speak."[3] Even the mask of hate merely increases the external distance without diminishing love's inner closeness. In fact, the mask of hate further intensifies her love: "I wanted you to think me odious,/I sought to appear inhuman in your eyes./To better resist your charm, I sought/To make you hate me. Oh, what useless care!/You hated me more. I loved you nonetheless./Your misfortunes only lent you added charm."[4] The concealed bond between Phaedra's fidelity and infidelity even turns her flight to her husband into a road to her beloved. Theseus's features mercilessly remind Phaedra of Hippolytus.[5] The sole goal and sole meaning of Phaedra's life have become a love whose fulfillment is refused not only by the outer world, by the beloved, and by Phaedra, but also by this love itself. For such a life, there is only one way out: death. When the tragedy commences, Phaedra is determined to take this way out.

2

As long as Phaedra protects the secret of her love, her flight from sin must appear as sin: against God, against Theseus, against her children.[6] Therefore, pressured by the nurse Oenone, Phaedra surrenders her secret. But her confession, made in order to be able to depart from life, compels her back into life and binds her in a series of events that allow her to die only after Hippolytus dies through her fault. Phaedra has scarcely confessed her love when she receives news of her husband's death. Instead of allowing her to die, Oenone convinces Phaedra that, for the sake of her defenseless children, she should not die; for the sake of her love, she must not die. The tragic unity of fidelity and infidelity, which until then had concealed her passion, now stands in her way through Oenone's practical politics: In order to secure Athens's throne for her children and not Aricia, Phaedra should form an alliance with Hippolytus. Thus, after months in exile, the unsuspecting Hippolytus reappears before Phaedra. Yet all her words are directed not toward her children but toward her beloved: They are first disguised as affirmations of her love for Theseus, whose ideal image stands before her, and then, when the fear of being understood gives way to the dread of not being understood, she openly confesses her love. Because Phaedra despises her passion, the confession of her love must culminate in the wish to be killed by her beloved. When Hippolytus refuses, she snatches his sword in despair so as to die by his weapon, only to be stopped by Oenone. The tragic in this scene is intensified by the news that reveals the supposed necessity of this meeting with Hippolytus to be a deception: Athens has already given preference to Phaedra's son as Theseus's successor. Oenone tries in vain to remind the queen of her duties, yet Hippolytus is now more than ever her only thought. Her confession not only strengthened her knowledge that her love cannot be fulfilled, but also shook it. Because Hippolytus knows of her love, the hope for its fulfillment has crept into her heart.[7] She explains his silence by reasoning that a man who grows up in the woods despises all women. To win him over, she is prepared to offer him Athens's throne. In her blindness, she beseeches help from the very goddess that she is a victim of: May Venus, out of revenge, convert Hippolytus to love. In tragic irony, her plea is fulfilled even before it is expressed. Hippolytus loves Aricia; the supposedly ambitious Hippolytus has renounced Athens's crown in favor of Aricia. At the only point in her tragic fate where she still remains hopeful, Phaedra is struck by the blow that robs her of all hope, even before she learns of Hippolytus's love. Sent to win over Hippolytus, Oenone returns with the message of Theseus's arrival. Like the wife in *The Imaginary Invalid*, Phaedra is unknowingly put to the test by fate. But Argan's cruel joke turns into the tragic, not least because Theseus's widow calls Hippolytus to her not to confess her love, but to secure the throne for Theseus's and her son. Once again it is Phaedra's fidelity that thrusts her onto the path of infidelity. Once again she is the wife of Theseus who wants to die out of her love for Hippolytus. But because she has betrayed her secret, she can now die only in disgrace. And once again, Oenone convinces the queen that, for the sake of her children, she cannot die, for the mother's sin would cast a shadow across their lives. What death means for Phaedra and what forbids her from dying thus again tragically coincide in disgrace. Paralyzed, Phaedra watches Oenone's intrigue. Like Iago, Oenone chooses as evidence for Hippolytus's guilt the object that proves his innocence: the sword he left in Phaedra's hands, because he (as Phaedra believes) did not want to defile himself with the weapon she touched. As soon as Oenone's plan is set into motion, Phaedra rushes after her to save Hippolytus. His rescue, however, is tragically thwarted by his own confession, which he sees as his salvation: the admission of his forbidden love for Aricia. Engulfed in doubt and falling prey to its dialectic, the saving moment doubly breaks down upon itself. Like Othello, Theseus looks only for evidence that demonstrates guilt, not innocence. And like Othello, he is more inclined to trust the object than the person: The evidence provided by the person tragically condemns itself, for it is all too believable and therefore appears to be deceptive. Theseus consequently refuses to believe his son's confession and beseeches his patron god to avenge him. Conversely, Phaedra is convinced (and for the same reason that Theseus is not) that what has been reported to her as Hippolytus's lie is true. Even for Phaedra, the dialectic of doubt holds true: What one fears appears to be more convincing than what one longs for. Despite Theseus's certainty, Phaedra no longer has the strength to doubt what she fears.[8] She therefore makes the extent of her suffering known for the first time. In the love between Aricia and Hippolytus, she sees everything granted that was denied to her, for Aricia's love is not only reciprocated, it is innocently reciprocated.[9] In her torment, Phaedra withholds the word that would save Hippolytus, and Hippolytus's confession, which should have exonerated him, turns against him a second time. Only now does Phaedra gain her freedom vis-à-vis Oenone. She kills herself, restoring to the world the pureness she had to destroy because she loved it. Her last word: "purity."

§ 18 *Demetrius*

Unlike Warbeck, his precursor in Schiller's last dramatic projects, who pretends to be the Duke of York, Demetrius is initially not a deceiver. By deciding to follow the historian Levesque and allowing Demetrius to believe that he is the lawful heir to the Russian throne, Schiller achieved what he could not seem to manage with Warbeck: the unity of subjective being and objective appearance that first enables the tragic treatment of the antagonism between being and appearance. Schiller thereby deepens the path of Demetrius's life into a path of consciousness. The first path, life's journey, leads Demetrius out of Sambor, where he lives as a Russian refugee with the Woiwoden family, and brings him first to the Reichstag in Krakow and then to Moscow as the leader of a Polish army unit. Along the second path, that of consciousness, Demetrius is taken out of a state of "harmless, happy ignorance"[1] and lifted into the imaginary heights of false consciousness, which takes appearance for being, only to be plunged into the abyss of true consciousness. True consciousness admittedly destroys Demetrius's false consciousness, but it cannot surrender the appearance that it has taken for reality and therefore devotes itself to untruthfulness. The two turning points in Demetrius's consciousness—when he is recognized as the czar's son and when he learns that he isn't it—are the foci of his tragic fate.

I

Salvation and annihilation are already tragically bound together in the prehistory of the first *peripeteia*, which follows a novel from La Rochelle. Because he wanted to protect himself from the jealous revenge of Palatinus (Marina's husband), Demetrius is threatened with capital punishment. What saves him from death—his being recognized as the czar's son—leads him along a path that will also inwardly destroy him, and with him, many others, such as Boris Gudunov. Yet the tragic dialectic that concerns Schiller's intellectual world first becomes visible in the motivation for this action. At the origin of this dialectic is not what one would call Demetrius's love for Woiwoden's daughter Marina. Rather, one finds in Schiller's notes that Demetrius's thoughts are directed toward her "more because his nature darkly strives for people like her than out of love for her."[2] Marina embodies for Demetrius the tragic power: "The Polish bride who initially grounds Demetrius's happiness also brings his misfortune with her."[3] But it is the deceptive voice of Demetrius's inner nature that attracts him to the one who, without his knowledge, will make him a deceiver. This voice feigns a noble descent and thus, instead of opposing truth to the external world of appearances, encourages Demetrius's step into the world of lies. Thus, from the beginning, Demetrius is the victim not only of circumstances, but also of himself. It is not only external signs that lead Demetrius to believe that he is the czar's son. When he learns in prison that he is Ivan's son, it is "as if a blindfold has fallen from his eyes. Everything obscure in his life suddenly receives light and significance."[4] Tragically originating in light, Demetrius's blindness is fostered by his ambition, his "enormous striving for the possible," that is "justified by a certain voice of the gods."[5] This phrase returns in Marina's line "May he / Follow the voice of the gods that drives him"[6] and is reminiscent of Schiller's last letter to Körner (April 25, 1805), where he calls *Demetrius* a companion piece to *The Maid of Orleans*. This is the case because in both plays, the voice of the gods thrusts someone out of nature's innocence, hurling both into the turmoil of history and ruining them. Yet this voice makes Joan of Arc a martyr, while it turns Demetrius into a deceiver and despot. Those surrounding Demetrius believe in him because "nature appears to have destined him for something higher."[7] "His higher spirit [stands] in contrast to his situation; . . . he has bodily strength, beauty, bold courage, esprit, insight, and magnanimity far beyond that of his class and fate."[8] Therefore, it is Demetrius's virtues that plummet him into deception and ruin. But more than his appearance and more than Marina's art of persuasion, Demetrius's own consciousness of himself assures the Poles and the Russians: "He believed in himself and thereby convinced the Woiwoden family;[9] Demetrius considers himself to be a czar and thereby becomes one."[10] Demetrius is led by his inner voice to a false consciousness that spreads into historical reality and turns it for the first time into a world of deception. All the tragic elements determining this first *peripeteia* share the fact that disaster comes from the very inner world of ideals, from the very voice of the heart and the gods, that Schiller otherwise considers to be the solitary source of salvation. The message of the poem "The Words of Delusion" appears to be revoked here. Demetrius's tragedy no longer lies in him listening to the words of delusion. It is not external reality that destroys a person who deludedly searched for the highest values "in the outer world." Rather, these values themselves become powers of destruction. The right that Demetrius finds in himself—following the poem's postulate—leads him and the outer world (which here is not hostile, but rather confirms his supposed mission) to ruin, for this right proves itself to be wrong. Demetrius's tragic experience is not that the earth does not belong to the good, for it is precisely his inner nobility that brings him his rule over the Russian earth. Nor is untruthfulness here—as the poem teaches—the work of earthly understanding: Only the calculating Marina and the clever statesman Sapieha do not succumb to the deception. The deception is, rather, the work of the faith inspired in Demetrius by the voice of his own nature and the gods. The first *peripeteia* thus mocks every aspect of the Idealism that the poem "The Words of Delusion" teaches. Yet the belief in "inner values" appears to be called into question not because this belief is subject to reality and its fortuitousness, but because it itself creates a reality to which it then falls victim. Nor can one conclude that Schiller has turned away from his faith from the fact that *Demetrius* gives form to the tragic aspect of Idealism. Rather, it is as if Schiller the Idealist became aware of the tragic potential of his position, as if Schiller the dramatist wanted to root the tragic in his own intellectual world.

2

"We rise after the fall"—this line from Gryphius[11] could stand as the motto over the path leading Demetrius from Sambor to Tula, from the first to the second of his turns of consciousness. "Demetrius's captivating happiness, in the face of which he himself gets dizzy. All hearts fall to his feet. . . . He is a god of mercy and grace for all; everything hopes in and greets the kingdom's new rising sun."[12] Yet the concealed destination of this ascent is Demetrius's fall into the abyss of deception from the heights of his supposedly legitimate claim to the throne. It is no accident that the initiator of this ascent, the "*fabricator doli*,"[13] faces Demetrius when he stands "upon the summit of happiness and favor."[14] But the *fabricator doli's* intention is to demand the reward for his "royal present"[15] to the future czar, whom he, the murderer of the true Demetrius, helped gain the throne. Every step Demetrius takes on his way to the czar's throne also leads him closer to self-knowledge and thus to his downfall. The tragic in this unity of rise and fall is intensified by the help Demetrius receives from Marina, the Polish nobility, and the czar's widow Marfa. This threefold help stems from the historical world of interests and purposes that Demetrius entered, at the cost of the world of love, during the first turning point of his path and changes into a threefold perniciousness. The "strength" of Marina's character, "which in the first act lifted up, bore, and curried favor with Demetrius, turns in the last act against him. In Marina, Demetrius only provided himself with a female tyrant."[16] The Polish army's help has the same result; their actions in Russia lead to the conspiracy that will cost Demetrius his life. Demetrius appears to intuit the danger when he reaches Russia's border: "Forgive me, precious ground, native soil. / You, sacred border marker that I grasp / And upon which my father carved his eagle, / Forgive me, that I, your son, disrupt / Your calm temple's peace with enemy weapons."[17] Demetrius can become czar only with the help of the Polish army, yet it is precisely this help that alienates him from his people. The tragic is already implanted in Demetrius's deception, in his belief that he is the rightful successor to the throne, and would destroy him even if he were the true Demetrius. Even Marfa's help is determined not by love, but by a lust for revenge. Before she sees Demetrius for the first time, she says: "And if he is not the son of my heart, then let him be the son of my revenge. I accept him as the one that heaven vengefully bore to me."[18] In Tula, she shows herself to the people by his side; her silence, which will expose Demetrius in Moscow, is here ironically sufficient to pronounce him to be the czar's son. Yet as soon as Marfa's lust for revenge is satisfied through Boris's death, she turns away from the son of her revenge and hands him over to the conspirators. Boris Godunov is not only Demetrius's political adversary, but also his counterimage in Schiller's anthropology. In clear contrast, for example, to *Mary Stuart*, in which the two queens are characterized by a similar equilibrium, the opposition of characters in *Demetrius* is subject to the principle of change. Mary and Elisabeth are, admittedly, not opposed like light and shadow. Yet in *Demetrius*, these two differently tinted shades of chiaroscuro are replaced by a light that darkens itself and a shadow that can struggle through to the light, but cannot outshine the darkness from which it stems and that finally falls prey to this darkness. Compared with Demetrius, the unknowingly deceptive claimant to the throne, Boris embodies neither the legitimate czar nor the criminal usurper. Rather, like Demetrius, Boris pursues a course, yet in the opposite direction. Although Boris became czar at the price of a criminal act, he can counter Demetrius's empty demands with his merits: "By making himself the ruler through *nefas*, he took on and *achieved* all the duties of the ruler; in the eyes of the people, he is an esteemed prince and a true father."[19] What Demetrius one day wants to become, Boris already is; what Demetrius after the second *peripeteia* must become, Boris was and no longer is. Whereas his own belief turns Demetrius the Idealist into a deceiver and a despot, Boris the czar can purify himself into the pure embodiment of the image of the father. Boris's tragic fate is not that the good leads him onto the path of evil, but rather that, even at the end of the path that led him to the good, he must pay for the evil from which he began. It is the tragic fate of the Realist.

3

A sketch from Schiller's posthumous writings provides an insight into the scene of Demetrius's second turn of consciousness. The prose, if only for a moment, offers consolation for the fact that Schiller was unable to complete the tragedy:

> When Demetrius has learned his true birth and convinced himself that he is not the true Demetrius (this happens immediately before a scene in which he needs to believe in himself more than ever), he first becomes silent and then poses a few short questions, hollow and cold—he then appears to quickly take sides and, partly in rage, partly with deliberation and prudence, he kills the messenger just as the latter mentions the expected reward—death is this reward. "You have pierced the heart of my life, you have stolen my faith in myself—Courage and hope, be gone. Joyful self-confidence, be gone! Joy! Trust and faith!—I have been trapped in a lie, I have been at odds with my very self! I am an enemy of humanity; the truth and I are separated forever!—What? Should I rudely awaken the people from their error? These great nations believe in me. Should I plummet them into disaster, into anarchy, and strip them of their belief? Should I expose myself as a deceiver?—I must go forward. I must remain steadfast, and yet I can no longer do this through my own inner conviction. Murder and blood must maintain me in my position.—How should I approach the czaress? How should I enter Moscow among the cheers of people with this lie in my heart?"
>
> As one enters, one sees the czar with the dagger and the dead man stretched out and steps back in disgust. This sight, immediately before Demetrius's entry as czar, holds a sinister significance.—He intuits everything that one can think of the situation and answers it, as well. He is no longer the old Demetrius; a tyrannical spirit has entered him. But he now also appears to be more terrible and more than a ruler. His evil conscience proves itself by him demanding more and acting more despotically. The dark suspicion already falls upon him; he doubts others because he no longer believes in himself.[20]

The words of the *fabricator doli* are first followed by silence, a sign of the gap that opens up between what Demetrius was and what he will become. Out of this emptiness, Demetrius regains himself, yet changed, and deliberately kills for the first time. Instead of rewarding the messenger, he punishes him with death. Yet Demetrius does not punish the messenger for deceiving him, but rather because he allowed himself to be deceived, because the messenger revealed how he, Demetrius, had deceived himself. "The heart of his life," which the *fabricator doli* pierces, is Demetrius's faith in himself. This faith is not merely Demetrius's belief that he is Ivan's son, but also something that first led him to this belief: the faith in the inner voice, the "confidence in himself," the trust in the world of ideals. Demetrius's lament and hate are directed, therefore, less toward the external world and more toward his inner world: From now on, he is at odds not with the world around him, but with himself. Demetrius then turns his attention to the present. Just as he is about to tear through the web of lies and confess his true birth, Demetrius realizes that he must maintain the deception if he is not to bring ruin upon those that believe in him. If in the past the good tragically changed into the ruinous for Demetrius, a different form of the tragic awaits him now, for the good simultaneously appears as ruinous and the ruinous as good. Unknowingly turned into a deceiver by his heart's voice, Demetrius shall now deliberately deceive: He must do what he is not allowed to do. At the "crossroads of two necessities,"[21] Demetrius does not realize that the two paths, between which he thinks he can choose, are in truth blocked. But blinded by the ambition inspired by the voice of the gods, Demetrius decides to follow the path of deception. Yet just as he reaches his decision, what enabled his ascent reverses in terrible irony and turns against him. Whereas the people believed in Demetrius because he believed in himself, doubt in others now creeps into his heart, for he can no longer believe in himself. He becomes the "horrible despot" of the very people he wanted to save and becomes this in a tragic manner: precisely through the "lie in his heart," the price that he was ready to pay for saving them. As a tyrant, Demetrius "loses both love and happiness"[22]—with this, his life is now forfeited.

In two notes that were to be kept in the completed play, Schiller's drafts go beyond the death of Demetrius. After Demetrius's murder, a Cossack remains behind "who knew how to obtain the czar's seal or accidentally obtained it." "With this seal," the Cossack sees "a means of playing Demetrius's person." He closes the tragedy with a monologue in which he "looks into a new series of storms; and the old, so to speak, begins anew."[23] These real events within the historical play are confronted by Romanov's vision, which history will prove to be right. In prison, Romanov learns of his appointment as czar with the instruction to let "fate ripen calmly."[24] With the new antagonists, Romanov and the second Demetrius, the old begins anew, but in a fundamentally different way. Demetrius lives on not only in the deceiver, but also in Romanov. The latter, however, embodies the "most charming and magnificent youth" that Demetrius was when he appeared in Sambor.[25] Regardless of the storms that may still be approaching, the horizon is no longer tragic. In Romanov and the Cossack, truth and deception, nobility and malice, are now forever distinguished: They are no longer the beginning and end of the same path, the path that Demetrius's tragic fate had to follow.

§ 19 *The Schroffenstein Family*

Although it is unsuccessful as poetry, Kleist's first drama is perhaps the boldest of his tragic conceptions. The drafts of *Robert Guiscard* (after whose completion Kleist planned to take his life) were repeatedly destroyed, and the works that establish Kleist's standing as a writer are indebted to renunciation, whether through his turn to comedy (in whose wings tragedy admittedly lurks) or through his defusing of the tragic, as *The Prince of Homburg* attests. Only in *Penthesilea* did Kleist remain faithful to the relentlessness of his earlier thought.

I

Modeled on Shakespeare's *Romeo und Juliet*, Kleist's *The Schroffenstein Family* uses a similar central theme: the love between children of parents who are enemies. The tragic unity of enmity and love—that as children of their parents the lovers must hate each other—defines both works. But from the beginning, Kleist exceeds Shakespeare in tragic acuteness, for he replaces the two antagonistic families with two houses of a single family, the Rossitzes and the Warwands. The discord thus has concord at its origin. It is not the feud that first ties the families together, as with Shakespeare's Montagues and Capulets. Rather, the strife binds and divides what was once united in love. In the two hostile houses, one family tree breaks apart and is threatened with destruction. Thus, the relationship between hate and love also changes. Hate and love no longer accidentally meet and are no longer differentiated according to whether the lovers view themselves in their ties to their parents or to one another. Rather, the love between the children appears where love once prevailed between the parents. It is not chance that sends love into the realm of discord, but the task of restoring concord. The mother of the Rossitz family says to the father: "O, put an end/To this wretched, evil strife/That threatens to wipe out the entire/Schroffenstein family except for the name./God is showing you the path to reconciliation./The children are in love."[1] The tragic in the failure that is love's destiny is measured both according to its inner and its outer task. Love is not just forbidden to assert itself in the midst of enmity; by attempting to save what is endangered, love brings about the catastrophe itself.

2

In Kleist, the repression of love and its utopian purpose have traits grounded in the philosophy of history. Rupert's words go beyond the fate of the Schroffenstein family, for they allow the state of the world to be read from this fate as if it were a model: "Nothing more of nature./It is a lovely, captivating fairy tale told/To children, to humanity, by poets and wet nurses./Trust, innocence, fidelity, love,/Religion, and fear of god are like/Animals that talk.—Even the bond,/The holy bond of blood relations is torn,/And cousins, children of one father, aim,/With daggers they aim at each other's breasts."[2] Love has disappeared from a world that alienated itself from nature. The world has replaced the natural tie with a contract that, like the apple from the tree of knowledge, becomes the origin of a fall from grace. The two counts' houses enter into a testamentary contract "by virtue of which, after one house/Entirely dies out, the entire property/Of the same shall fall upon the other house."[3] This contract, rather than love, now binds the Rossitzes and the Warwands, and the bond is called enmity. The contract has permanently arranged what the heart should always achieve anew. In Kleist's eyes, this turning away from nature in favor of the letter is the sin that is punished with downfall. The testamentary contract itself embodies the tragic moment, for the two houses entered into it not out of discord, but in concord. Its purpose is to safeguard the family property. But through its form as a contract, it thwarts what it aspires to in content. Instead of preserving the Schroffenstein estate and putting things right were one house to die out, the contract itself causes both houses to die out.

3

The weapon that the testamentary contract places in man's hands is mistrust. Every action is distorted by mistrust's radioactive field and thus appears as a criminal act committed out of the desire to realize what the testamentary contract posited as a possible disaster. Like Iago's irony, mistrust changes good into evil: "Mistrust is the black addiction of the soul, / And for the sick eye, everyone, even the innocently pure, / Wears the traditional garb of hell."[4] In its self-relation, mistrust also possesses a dialectical nature. What mistrust fears and seeks to thwart, it brings about itself. Rupert says: "In advance they branded me / A murderer, maliciously.—Well, / Then they will have been right."[5] The one who is first suspected of being a murderer truly becomes a murderer; the supposed revenge for murder first leads to murder. Ottokar and Agnes must die, for under a cloud of mistrust their brothers' deaths appear to be murder. The mistrust of the one who is not entirely blind turns against him, not first in the act, but already in considering the act. Sylvester realizes that he cannot hold Johann (who drew a dagger against his daughter) for a killer hired by Rupert, even when Johann names Rupert upon being tortured, because Rupert considers Sylvester to be his son's murderer for the same reason: the man Rupert met holding a bloody knife by his son's corpse named Sylvester under torture. And the event that Gertrude reminds Sylvester of to strengthen his suspicion that Rupert poisoned their son equally turns against her. If she is right, then Sylvester, who remembers the incident better, would have been poisoned back then not by Rupert's wife, but by his own wife, Gertrude.[6]

4

If there were a form of certain knowledge, mistrust could not take up its rule. But it is precisely knowledge that is denied to the Schroffensteins. By leaving the state of nature and entering into that of contractual agreements, they forfeited their only possibility of certain knowledge: the heart. The unreliability of the faculty of knowledge would not be tragic if one could orient his actions in accordance with some other power. But unlike the children, who love one another, the parents know nothing but this faculty. They must, therefore, depend on something they cannot depend upon, for there is no action that does not follow the inner voice or what it considers to be the indication of reality. In Kleist, however, the signs that the world of appearances gives to man to help him find his way always lead him astray. The more unambiguous the signs appear to be, the more they lead astray. Neither mimicry nor gesture speaks a clear language. Ottokar says: "Facial expressions / Are bad riddles that refer to no one thing."[7] When Johann draws his dagger so that Agnes, who doesn't return his love, will kill him, he is caught in this pose and thought to be a murderer. Nor can one even rely on a word's meaning. When a word seems to be most unambiguous—that is, in the proper name—it deceives the most. Rupert names Sylvester with great emphasis in his pledge of revenge. But the revenge recoils upon Rupert, for he let himself be deceived by Sylvester's name when the one being tortured named it. The entire community may have heard the name be spoken and, like Rupert, may believe in Sylvester's guilt, yet their tumult in the marketplace during the torture simultaneously prevented them from hearing more than the mere name from the confession. Thus, even in the evidence of Sylvester's guilt, what substantiates it and what questions it coincide. Rupert, however, trusts only this one name and marches on to his supposed revenge, which will first make murderers of him and those on whom he seeks revenge.

5

The lovers form a world of their own in this hostile environment; their task is to resist and to redeem the environment. Fortune and fear, trust and suspicion, knowledge and deception fight against each other in the conversations between Agnes and Ottokar. Only with difficulty can they free themselves from the tentacles of enmity and blindness and find one another in truth. Salvation and destruction are still entwined in the scene where Ottokar offers Agnes water from the spring. After fainting from the sudden knowledge of Ottokar's origin, Agnes believes that the drink he gives her is poisoned. She drinks it, however, out of the desire to die, because she assumes that Ottokar, whom she loves, wants her death. Only gradually does the heart's knowledge break through the external world's deceiving semblance. Agnes says of this knowledge: "For there is something far beyond all imagining and knowing—/The feeling of the goodness of another's soul."[8] In this feeling, which is knowledge, man climbs over the gap that separates him from the other—for Kleist, love and knowledge become again the synonyms they once were. The final scene of the tragedy (which in the history of its origin is its nucleus) is dedicated to one person transforming into the other.[9] The scene gives form to the two fundamental themes of Kleist's entire writing in their tragic context: what divides people and the difficulty of knowledge. Ottokar and Agnes meet in a mountain cavern located between the estates of Rossitz and Warwand, between the two enemies whose children they are. Here they withdraw into their inner realm. Knowing of the threat posed to Agnes by his father, Ottokar disrobes her "of her alien covering"[10] and, to deceive Rupert, gives her his own clothes, putting on hers. Thus, the union and mutual transformation of the two lovers take place in the medium that divides them and differentiates them in the eyes of their fathers, who can judge only appearances. But their love thereby turns from salvation to ruin. Instead of overcoming the fathers' blindness and saving lovers and enemies alike from demise, love itself becomes the force that enables the blindness to complete its dreadful work. Under the delusion of killing Sylvester's daughter, Rupert kills his own son. Thinking Ottokar murdered his daughter, Sylvester pounces upon the one wearing Ottokar's clothes and thereby kills his own daughter, whose death he wants to avenge. The clothes that were meant to save Agnes become her downfall, just as the love that is supposed to conquer enmity becomes its cruel accomplice and avenger in one. Although the fathers, now awakened to the truth, shake hands in reconciliation at the end, Johann (Rupert's natural son, who, as such, isn't affected by the testamentary contract and is therefore a child of nature) goes out of his mind because of the unnatural world. He thereby bathes this harmonious scene, which is achieved too late, in a mad twilight that recalls Shakespeare. In speaking to Ursula, who stands at the origin of the tragic deception and is a sister of the witches in *Macbeth*, Johann uses words defined by a cruel irony that transforms evil back into good after good tragically became evil: "Go, old witch, go./You play a good trick/I am satisfied with it, go."[11]

§ 20 *Danton's Death*

I

Büchner's play is the tragedy of the revolutionary. Danton does not die as a martyr of the revolution; he is its victim. The revolution destroys the revolutionary who seeks to prevent its turning into tyranny. Tragically uniting creation and destruction, the relation between revolution and tyranny recalls the one between father and son that forms the basis of *Oedipus Rex*. The mythical intensification of the historical, however, is already executed in Büchner's play. Danton says: "The revolution is like Saturn, it eats its own children."[1] Believing or pretending to believe in the significance of these victims, Saint-Just compares the revolution to Pelias's daughters in a speech before the National Assembly that is to condemn Danton: "The revolution tears humanity into small pieces in order to rejuvenate it."[2] But the irony of the comparison is overlooked or kept silent, for the daughters of the king of Jolkos were the victims of Medea's diabolical advice. Deluded into believing that they were rejuvenating their father, they killed him. The conversion of salvation into ruin, which also characterizes the historical events, is moored in the antithetical structure of the revolution itself. The revolution is simultaneously based on love and hate. Because virtue must bring terror into its service, it necessarily turns into its opposite. Initially destroying so as to help, the revolution ultimately destroys because it cannot help. A mother at the Place de la Revolution calls out during Danton's execution: "Make room! Make room! The children are screaming because they are hungry. I have to let them watch so that they will be quiet. Make room!"[3] The guillotine was supposed to abolish class differences and make the republic possible. Now, following Mercier's saying,[4] the revolution republicanizes by no longer differentiating between nobility and revolutionaries: both are its victims. The irony of this statement leaps over the tragic opposition between intention and reality by referring to their identical effects. It thereby illuminates all the more piercingly the dialectical process that leads the revolutionary to the revolution's guillotine. Additionally, the moderate Danton must fall because the radical Hébertists were executed, a fact that could awaken in the people the suspicion of moderation: Danton, a tragic hero, thus dies more for the opposition's cause than for his own. The tragic inherent in the historical events is further intensified in Büchner's interpretation of them. The "horrible fatalism of history," which makes Büchner feel "as if destroyed,"[5] does not mean that the revolution is condemned to failure due to man's inability to fight against the existing powers. Rather, the revolution fails because it cannot free itself from the spell of "necessity" and, indeed, is based upon it, just like the conditions it wants to abolish. Although the revolution wrote "freedom" on its flag, it did not originate in the free decision of the revolutionaries. "We did not make the revolution, the revolution made us,"[6] says Danton, in whose comparison of the revolution with Saturn, the revolution already played the role of the destroying creator and not that of the created. This quote from Danton also shows his tragic fate from another side, for it raises the question of the type of man that the revolution has made out of him. "Danton has beautiful clothes, Danton has a beautiful house, Danton has a beautiful wife, he bathes in burgundy, eats his game from silver plates, and sleeps with your wives and daughters when he is drunk."[7] Uttered in the plaza in front of the Palace of Justice, these are the words a citizen uses to describe Danton, whose fate is sealed when the people reply by calling out "Down with the traitor!" This description concludes, however, with a demagogic *argumentum ad hominem*, so that the people do not notice that its beginning is filled with desire for the very happiness promised to all by the revolution and apparently already granted to Danton. Danton says that the people "hate those who enjoy life like a eunuch hates men."[8] What Robespierre calls Danton's vice is the excessive pleasure in beauty and happiness that he and his friends do not want to relinquish and that the people do not desire any less. Danton thus succumbs not merely to the revolution, but also to the revolutionary victory that he has already gained. He is a traitor not because he joined forces with the king and foreign countries (as the people suspect), but because in the frenzy of destruction he has remained true to the happiness that he would not begrudge to anyone, although he enjoys it before others do.

2

But the play is more than the tragedy of the revolutionary. Not only does Danton the revolutionary fall prey to the revolution, but Danton the man falls prey to himself. In the two scenes preceding his arrest, Danton beats to the punch the enemies who condemn him to death. The scene entitled "Open Field" stands out from the others both in its monologue form and in its location. More importantly, with the fleeing Danton stopping his flight and turning back, this scene presents the drama's *peripeteia* and offers an insight into Danton's fate, which frees his tragic end from the theme of revolution. On the way to his hiding place, he gains an insight into his situation: "The place should be safe, at least for my memory, but not for me; the grave offers me more security, it at least allows me *to forget*. It kills my memory. The hiding place allows my memory to live and kills me."[9] The unity of salvation and annihilation, which tragedy usually proves in the plot's unfolding, is here, as it were, momentarily recognized in a condensed form in reflection. The flight that would save Danton from his enemies would simultaneously be his destruction, for it would save the enemy he bears within himself. "Then I ran like a Christian to save an enemy, that is, my memory." The tragic paradox of Danton's lot is characterized by the fact that the flight from his inner enemy excludes the flight from his external enemy. He has nothing in common with the criminal who succeeds in escaping his pursuer only to be judged by his own conscience. Danton does not reproach himself for his depravity, a depravity that will lead him to the guillotine, but rather for his role in the September murders. For his executioners, Danton's role is a meritorious act, not a guilty one, and should protect him from being executed. The intertwining of salvation and destruction is thus crystallized not merely in Danton's flight, but also in the deeds whose memory Danton flees. Estranged as hallucinations, these deeds pursue him at night as

"September" screams. In his conversation with Julie, Danton attempts to convince himself that those murders were necessary. But his knowledge of the compulsion that is said to guide all human action bars him from tracing the rescue of the fatherland through the murder of royalist and clerical prisoners back to his free decision. He therefore cannot decide whether the murders were justified or not. "What is that in us that lies, whores, steals, and murders?" Danton asks with words also found in Büchner's letter that speaks of the fatalism of history. It is just as little Danton's own decision to summon the past to appear before the tribunal of his conscience. In a conversation with Robespierre, he called the conscience a "mirror before which an ape torments itself."[10] His insight into "necessity"[11] cannot calm him, for he recognizes that it causes not only his actions, but also his memory, which is as foreign to him as the murders it judges. Danton therefore refuses to use the name "conscience" to describe "necessity." To not become his own murderer, Danton flees from his inner struggle (which he cannot take part in) to his murderers.

3

Danton's turning back on the path that leads from a saving destruction to a destroying salvation is accompanied by two factors that decisively change his tragic end. The fleeing Danton longs for the death that awaits him in Robespierre's Paris and simultaneously refuses to believe entirely in this death. Along with the historical words "They would not dare to," Büchner's hero says: "There is a feeling of permanence in me that says: Tomorrow will be like today, and the day after tomorrow the same; everything is as it was."[12] The feeling of always the same that guarantees the continuation of Danton's life, however, is in tragic fashion the same boredom that expels him from life. The tragic in his deception consists not only in the fact that it occurs through a feeling he heeds as if it were the reliable feeling of nature, but also in the fact that he heeds it at all. The excessive lucidity of his consciousness, the demand for a knowledge that penetrates all things, has long since alienated Danton from his feelings. To Julie's question whether he believes in her, Danton answers: "What do I know? We know little about one another. . . . Know one another? We would have to crack open the tops of our skulls and tear out each other's thoughts from the fibers of our brains."[13] By making the destruction of the beloved the condition of knowing the beloved, this sentence in the drama's first scene already refers to Danton's death. Before his enemies enter the scene, before the memory of the September murders descends upon him, Danton's life is forfeited. It has become a life that is no longer livable. As the decision of the Committee of Public Safety is made known, Danton does not hide his feelings: "They want my head; Let them have it."[14] Despite Danton's consent to his demise, his fate remains a tragic one. If this consent weakens the tragic nature of his death by indicating that it is desired, it also strengthens the tragic nature of his life, which had to turn against itself. Danton says: "Life is not worth the work one does to maintain it."[15] Yet for the living Danton, this work is regarded as life itself. The unity of life and work is first divided into means and ends in the estranged gaze of Danton, whom knowledge has already lifted out of life prior to his death. Danton shares this gaze—a gaze that no longer understands life because it has understood it—with most tragic heroes, such as Hamlet, with whom Danton is often compared. The duty of avenging his father, however, estranges Hamlet from the world, while it is precisely the strangeness of the world that prevents Danton from still believing in duty. Both are knowledgeable and sacrifice their life to knowledge. But Hamlet knows of a crime that must be punished, while Danton thinks he knows about life itself. His knowledge devalues and destroys, regardless of whether it penetrates the world or ricochets off it. In Danton's view, both the deciphered and the enigma are empty and dead. Danton says to Lacroix: "You called me a dead saint. You were more right than you thought."[16] And later: "We are buried alive and, like kings, interred in three- or four-layered coffins: under the heavens, in our houses, in our skirts and shirts.—We scratch for fifty years on the coffin lid."[17] Danton's tragic fate is not that life's contradictions drive him to death, but rather that death comes into conflict with his life on his life's own ground. Danton suffers from the antagonism between a body that is active and a spirit that passively watches it,[18] between the love for another life and the knowledge that destroys this beloved life. Only through this tragic self-dissolution of life does pleasure alone assume the throne and that Epicurean saying originate to which Danton declares his allegiance in desperate pride. But since death is now implanted in life itself, death can no longer be the exit that tragic heroes otherwise rush toward in blind clairvoyance. The work is called *Danton's Death* not only because it presents the last days of its hero, but also because death (which is often automatically identified as the formal element in tragic literature) has become problematic. In contrast to Phaedra, Hamlet, and Demetrius, whose deaths do not need to be named in the title, Danton is characterized less by the fact that he must die and more by the fact that he cannot die, for he is already dead. There is no way out of a life that experiences itself as being dead[19]: Its end is the guillotine that finds the body of the hero as motionless as if he were already dead. Under the guillotine, Büchner's hero arrives at a heightened expression of himself: Danton's death is Danton's life.[20]

Notes

Translator's note: Unless an English-language edition is cited for translations of German texts, all such translations are mine. Existing translations have been slightly modified. In the chapters on Sophocles and Calderon, I have translated the German editions used by Szondi and have provided existing English translations in the endnotes. Szondi quotes Shakespeare and Racine in their original languages without providing the editions used.

Introduction

1. Cf. Emil Staiger's reference to this point in *Der Geist der Liebe und das Schicksal* (Leipzig: Frauenfeld, 1935), p. 41. Also, Friedrich T. Vischer: "An aesthetic system first became possible with Schelling, for he first took up the position of the idea again." *Über das Erhabene und Komische*, in *Kritische Gänge*, 2d edition, edited by Robert Vischer (Munich: Meyer and Jesson, 1920–22), vol. 4, p. 8.

2. Cf. Max Kommerell, *Lessing und Aristotle: Untersuchungen über die Theorie der Tragödie* (Frankfurt am Main: Klostermann, 1940).

3. Miguel de Unamuno, *Das tragische Lebensgefühl* (Munich: Meyer and Jessen, 1925); *Tragic Sense of Life*, translated by J. E. Crawford Flitch (New York: Dover Publications, 1954).

4. [In this sentence and throughout this book, Szondi uses two terms for the tragic—*das Tragische* and *die Tragik*—both expressing the whole of the tragic process. Both words normally will be rendered as "the tragic" throughout the translation. In a few cases, however, it was necessary to "unpack" the term and, depending upon the context, to render it as "the tragic process," "the tragic fate," "the tragic aspect," and so on—trans.]

5. Marcel Proust, in a letter to Sidney Schiff, *Correspondance générale* (Paris: Plon, 1932), vol. 3, p. 31.

6. Cf. G. W. F. Hegel, *Rechtsphilosophie*, in *Jubiläums Ausgabe*, edited by Hermann Glockner (Stuttgart: Friedrich Frommanns Verlag, 1958), vol. 7, p. 37; *Elements of the Philosophy of Right*, translated by H. S. Nisbet (Cambridge: Cambridge University Press, 1991), p. 23.

Chapter 1

1. F. W. J. Schelling, *Briefe über Dogmatismus und Kritizismus*, in *Hauptwerke der Philosophie in originalgetreuen Neudrucken* (Leipzig: F. Müller Verlag, 1914), p. 85. *Philosophical Letters on Dogmatism and Criticism*, in *The Unconditional in Human Knowledge: Four Early Essays, 1794–1796*, translated by Fritz Marti (Lewisburg, Pa.: Bucknell University Press, 1980), pp. 192–93. Cf. Emil Staiger, *Der Geist der Liebe und das Schicksal*, p. 41.

2. Johann Gottlieb Fichte, *Grundlage der gesamten Wissenschaftslehre*, in *Werke*, edited by F. Medicus (Leipzig: Fritz Eckart Verlag, 1911), vol 1., p. 295; *Science of Knowledge*, translated by Peter Heath and John Lachs (New York: Meredith Corporation, 1970), p. 102.

3. *Aus Schellings Leben*, edited by Gustav Plitt (Leipzig: S. Hirzel Verlag, 1869), vol. 1, pp. 76–77.

4. Ibid.

5. Schelling, *Briefe*, p. 84; Marti, p. 192.

6. Ibid., p. 85; Marti, p. 192.

7. Ibid., p. 88; Marti, p. 194.

8. Throughout this book, the words "dialectic" and "dialectical" adhere to Hegel's usage and designate (without the implications of his system) the following elements and processes: the unity of opposites, the change into one's opposite, the negative positing of oneself, self-division.

9. F. W. J. Schelling, *Philosophie der Kunst*, in *Werke* (Stuttgart: J. G. Cotta, 1856–61), pt. 1, vol. 5, p. 693; *The Philosophy of Art*, translated by Douglas W. Stott (Minneapolis: University of Minnesota Press, 1989), p. 251.

10. Ibid., p. 696; Stott, p. 253.

11. Ibid., p. 380; Stott, p. 28.

12. Ibid., p. 383; Stott, p. 30.

13. Ibid., p. 687; Stott, p. 247.

Chapter 2

1. Friedrich Hölderlin, *Sämtliche Werke: Große Stuttgarter Ausgabe*, edited by Friedrich Beißner (Stuttgart: J. G. Cottasche Buchhandlung, 1943–85), vol. 4, p. 274; *Sämtliche Werke: Historisch-kritische Ausgabe*, edited by L. v. Pigenot (Berlin: Propyläen, 1943), vol. 3, p. 275; "The Significance of

Tragedies," *Friedrich Hölderlin: Essays and Letters on Theory*, translated by Thomas Pfau (Albany: State University of New York Press, 1988), p. 89. "By way of paradox" in line one is the variant interpretation of Zinkernagel and Beißner, cf. *Zum Hölderlin-Text: Neue Lesarten zu einigen theoretischen Aufsätze*, in *Dichtung und Volkstum* (Frankfurt am Main: Klostermann, 1938). According to Pigenot, the text begins "The ('proper' crossed out) significance of all tragedies is explained by way of the paradoxes that everything original—because everything good is divided justly and equally—does not truly appear, but rather, properly, only in its own weakness" (vol. 3, p. 589). In line four, "quite" (*recht*) is Zinkernagel's and Beißner's variant interpretation, whereas Pigenot and Böhm read "indeed" (*wohl*).

2. [Through an analysis of the handwriting, diction, and the paper's watermarks, the *Frankfurter Hölderlin-Ausgabe* has recently shown that this fragment was actually written in 1803. See vol. 14, edited by D. E. Sattler and Wolfram Groddeck (Frankfurt am Main: Verlag Roter Stern, 1979), p. 193—trans.]

3. *Große Stuttgarter Ausgabe*, vol. 6, p. 329.

4. Ibid., vol. 6, p. 300.

5. Ibid., vol. 4, p. 154; Pfau, pp. 54–55.

6. Ibid., vol. 4, p. 156 f.; Pfau, p. 56.

7. Ibid., vol. 4, p. 147; Pfau, p. 57.

8. Ibid.

9. Ibid., vol. 5, p. 201; Pfau, p. 107.

10. Ibid., vol. 5, p. 202; Pfau, p. 108.

11. Ibid., vol. 5, p. 197; Pfau, p. 102.

Chapter 3

1. G. W. F. Hegel, *Über die wissenschaftlichen Behandlungsarten des Naturrechts, seine Stelle in der praktischen Philosophie, und sein Verhältnis zu den positiven Rechtswissenschaften*, in *Jubiläums Ausgabe*, edited by Hermann Glockner (Stuttgart: Friedrich Frommanns Verlag, 1958), vol. 1, pp. 501–2; *The Scientific Ways of Treating Natural Law, Its Place in Moral Philosophy, and Its Relation to the Positive Sciences*, translated by T. M. Knox (Philadelphia: University of Pennsylvania Press, 1975), p. 105.

2. Ibid., p. 525; Knox, p. 124.

3. [Throughout the book, I will follow the standard English translation of Hegel's notion of *Sittlichkeit*, rendering it as either "ethics" or "ethical life"—trans.]

4. Ibid., p. 452; Knox, p. 66.

5. Ibid., p. 527; Knox, p. 125.

6. Ibid., p. 509 f.; Knox, p. 112.

7. Ibid., p. 500; Knox, p. 104.

8. Ibid., p. 501; Knox, p. 105.

9. *Hegels theologische Jugendschriften*, edited by Herman Nohl (Tübingen: J. C. B. Mohr, 1907), p. 283; *The Spirit of Christianity and Its Fate*, in *Early Theological Writings*, translated by T. M. Knox (Chicago: The University of Chicago Press, 1948), p. 232. [Szondi quotes here a passage that Hegel crossed out and that is therefore not found in Knox's edition—trans.]

10. Ibid., p. 392. [From a text not translated by Knox—trans.]

11. Ibid., p. 393 in footnote. [From a text not translated by Knox—trans.]

12. Ibid., p. 281; Knox, p. 230.

13. Ibid., p. 281; Knox, p. 230.

14. Ibid., p. 293; Knox, p. 244.

15. G. W. F. Hegel, *Über die wissenschaftlichen Behandlungsarten des Naturrechts*, p. 441.

16. G. W. F. Hegel, *Ästhetik*, in *Jubiläums Ausgabe*, vol. 14, p. 528; *Aesthetics*, translated by T. M. Knox (Oxford: Clarendon Press, 1975), vol. 2, pp. 1195–96.

17. Ibid., p. 567; Knox, vol. 2, p. 1226.

18. Ibid., p. 556; Knox, vol. 2, p. 1218.

19. This moment of sublation corresponds to the position of the classical (Greek) art form, which is located between the symbolic (including the Hebraic) and the romantic (Christian) art forms. Cf. *Ästhetik*, in *Jubiläums Ausgabe*, vol. 13, p. 15.

20. *Hegels theologische Jugendschriften*, p. 260; Knox, *The Spirit of Christianity*, p. 205.

21. Regarding Hegel, cf. also p. 51 of this book.

Chapter 4

1. Karl Wilhelm Ferdinand Solger, *Vorlesungen über Ästhetik*, edited by Karl Wilhelm Ludwig Heyse (Leipzig: F. A. Brockhaus, 1829), p. 309.

2. Ibid., p. 311.

3. Ibid., p. 310.

4. Solger, *Nachgelassene Schriften und Briefwechsel*, edited by Ludwig Tieck and Friedrich von Raumer (Leipzig: F. A. Brockhaus, 1826), vol. 2, p. 466.

5. *Vorlesungen*, p. 97.

6. Ibid., p. 77.

7. Ibid., p. 96.

Chapter 5

1. *Unterhaltungen mit Goethe*, edited by Ernst Grumach (Weimar: Böhlau, 1956), p. 118.

2. Goethe, in conversation with Eckermann, March 3, 1827.

3. In a letter to C. F. Zelter, dated October 31, 1831. *Goethes Werke, Sophien-Ausgabe* (Weimar: Böhlaus, 1909), pt. 4, vol. 49, p. 128.

4. *Goethes Werke, Propyläen-Ausgabe*, edited by Ernst Schukte-Strathaus (Munich: G. Müller, 1910), vol. 35, p. 84.

5. Ibid., vol. 26, p. 48.

6. Ibid., vol. 35, p. 84.

7. Ibid., vol. 33, p. 255.

8. Ibid., vol. 35, p. 190.

Chapter 6

1. Arthur Schopenhauer, *Sämtliche Werke*, edited by Arthur Hübscher (Leipzig: Brockhaus, 1938), vol. 2, p. 298–99; *The World as Will and Representation*, translated by E. F. J. Payne (New York: Dover, 1958), vol. 1, p. 253.

2. Ibid., vol. 3, p. 495; Payne, vol. 2, pp. 433–34.

3. Ibid., vol. 2, p. 216; Payne, vol. 1, p. 184.

4. Ibid., vol. 2, p. 323; Payne, vol. 1, p. 275.

5. Ibid., vol. 2, p. 217; Payne, vol. 1, pp. 184–85.

6. Ibid., vol. 2, p. 181; Payne, vol. 1, p. 152.

7. Ibid., vol. 2, p. 179; Payne, vol. 1, p. 150.

Chapter 7

1. Friedrich Theodor Vischer, *Über das Erhabene und Komische*, in *Kritische Gänge*, 2d edition, edited by Robert Vischer (München: Meyer and Jesson, 1920–22), vol. 4, pp. 63–64.

2. Ibid., vol. 4, p. 404.

3. Ibid., vol. 6, p. 472.

4. Cf. Ewald Volhard, *Zwischen Hegel und Nietzsche: Der Ästhetiker Friedrich Theodor Vischer* (Frankfurt am Main: Klostermann, 1932).

5. F. T. Vischer, *Kritische Gänge*, vol. 4, p. 28.

6. Ibid., p. 29.

7. Ibid., p. 65.

8. Ibid., p. 71.

9. Ibid., p. 89.

10. F. T. Vischer, *Ästhetik*, in *Kritische Gänge*, vol. 6, p. 275.

Chapter 8

1. Søren Kierkegaard, *Unwissenschaftliche Nachschrift*, in *Kierkegaard-Jubiläums-Ausgabe*, p. 709; *Concluding Unscientific Postscript*, translated by David F. Swenson and Walter Lowrie (Princeton: Princeton University Press, 1968), p. 459.

2. Ibid., p. 711; Swenson, p. 463.

3. Cf. p. 26 of this book.

4. Kierkegaard, *Entweder/Oder*, in *Gesammelte Werke*, translated by Emanuel Hirsch (Gütersloh: Gütersloher Verlagshaus Gerd Mohn, 1980), vol.

1, p. 175; *Either/Or*, translated by Howard V. Hong and Edna H. Hong (Princeton: Princeton University Press, 1987), vol. 1, p. 163.

5. Kierkegaard, *Die Krankheit zum Tode und anderes*, in *Jubiliäums-Ausgabe*, p. 245.

6. Kierkegaard, *Unwissenschaftliche Nachschrift*, p. 717 f.; Swenson, p. 464.

7. Kierkegaard, *Stadien auf dem Lebensweg*, in *Gesammelte Werke*, translated by Christoph Schremp (Jena: Eugen Diederichs, 1914), p. 414; *Stages on Life's Way*, translated by Walter Lowrie (Princeton: Princeton University Press, 1940), p. 405.

8. Kierkegaard, *Entweder/Oder*, vol. 1, p. 175; Hong, vol. 1, p. 164.

9. Kierkegaard, *Die Tagebücher*, 3rd edition, translated by Theodor Haecker (Munich: Kosel Verlag, 1949), p. 134.

10. Ibid., p. 248: "Since my earliest childhood an arrow of suffering is lodged in my heart. As long as it remains there, I am ironic—if it is removed, I die."

Chapter 9

1. Friedrich Hebbel, *Sämtliche Werke*, edited by Richard Maria Werner (Berlin: Behr Verlag, 1904), pt. 1, vol. 11, pp. 3–4.

2. Ibid., p. 29.

3. Hebbel, *Tagebücher*, in *Sämtliche Werke*, pt. 2, no. 2664.

4. Hebbel, *Sämtliche Werke*, pt. 1, vol. 11, p. 30.

5. Cf. Hebbel, *Tagebücher*, no. 988, 998, 1007 (on Solger) and *Briefwechsel*, edited by Felix Bamberg (Berlin: G. Grote Verlag, 1890), vol 1, pp. 107–8 (on Hegel).

6. Hebbel, *Tagebücher*, no. 2771.

7. Ibid., no. 1034.

8. Hebbel, *Sämtliche Werke*, pt. 1, vol. 11, p. 32.

9. Ibid., p. 31.

10. Hebbel, *Tagebücher*, no. 3088.

11. Hebbel, *Sämtliche Werke*, pt. 1, vol. 11, pp. 30–31.

12. Hebbel, *Tagebücher*, no. 2634, cf. no. 3168.

13. Ibid., no. 2721.

14. Cf. p. 51 of this book.

15. Hebbel, *Sämtliche Werke*, pt. 1, vol. 11, p. 61.

16. Hebbel, *Tagebücher*, no. 1012.

Chapter 10

1. Friedrich Nietzsche, *Werke* (Leipzig: Naumann, 1921), vol. 1, p. 194; *The Birth of Tragedy and The Case of Wagner*, translated by Walter Kaufmann (New York: Random House, 1967), section 24, p. 140.

2. Ibid., p. 64; Kaufmann, section 4, p. 46.
3. Ibid., p. 196; Kaufmann, section 24, pp. 140–42.
4. Ibid., p. 90; Kaufmann, section 8, pp. 64–65.
5. Ibid., p. 101; Kaufmann, section 10, p. 73.
6. Ibid.
7. Ibid., p. 102; Kaufmann, section 10, p. 74.

Chapter 11

1. Georg Simmel, "Der Begriff und die Tragödie der Kultur," in *Logos II* (Tübingen: J. C. B. Mohr, 1912), pp. 21–22; also in *Philosophische Kultur* (Leipzig: Klinkhardt Verlag, 1911).
2. Wilhelm Dilthey, *Gesammelte Schriften*, edited by Martin Redeker and Ulrich Herrmann (Berlin: B. G. Teubner, 1921), vol. 8, p. 71.
3. Simmel, "Der Begriff und die Tragödie der Kultur," p. 1.
4. Ibid., p. 6.
5. Ibid., p. 25.
6. Georg Simmel, *Fragmente und Aufsätze aus dem Nachlaß und Veröffentlichungen der letzten Jahren* (Munich: Drei Masken Verlag, 1923), p. 115.
7. Ibid., p. 113.
8. Ibid., p. 20.

Chapter 12

1. Max Scheler, "Zum Phänomen des Tragischen," in *Vom Umsturz der Werte: Abhandlungen und Aufsätze. Gesammelte Werke* (Bern: Francke Verlag, 1955), vol. 3, p. 155.
2. Ibid., p. 158.
3. Max Scheler, *Der Formalismus in der Ethik und die materiale Wertethik* (Halle: Niemeyer, 1913), p. 160; *Formalism in Ethics and Non-Formal Ethics of Value*, translated by Manfred S. Frings and Roger L. Funk (Evanston, Ill.: Northwestern University Press, 1973), p. 159.
4. Ibid., p. 10; Frings, p. 15.
5. Karl Jaspers writes in a similar vein: "The tragic is when each of the colliding powers is true for itself." "Über das Tragische," in *Von der Wahrheit* (Munich: Piper Verlag, 1952), p. 29.
6. Scheler, "Zum Phänomen des Tragischen," p. 153.
7. Ibid., p. 159.

Transition

1. As is the case, for example, in Otto Mann's *Poetik der Tragödie* (Bern:

Francke Verlag, 1958), which opposes the "speculations" of the very thinkers addressed in the commentaries presented here.

2. Walter Benjamin, *Ursprung des deutschen Trauerspiels*, in *Gesammelte Schriften*, edited by Rolf Tiedemann and Hermann Schweppenhäuser (Frankfurt am Main: Suhrkamp, 1974), vol. 1, pt. 1, p. 214; *The Origin of German Tragic Drama*, translated by John Osborne (New York: Verso, 1977), p. 34.

3. Ibid., pp. 285–86; Osborne, pp. 106–7.

4. Ibid., p. 286; Osborne, p. 107.

5. Ibid.

6. Walter Benjamin, "Schicksal und Charakter," in *Gesammelte Schriften*, edited by Rolf Tiedemann and Hermann Schweppenhäuser (Frankfurt am Main: Suhrkamp, 1974), vol. 2, pt. 1, pp. 171–79; "Fate and Character," in *Reflections*, translated by Edmund Jephcott (New York: Schocken Books, 1978), pp. 304–11.

7. Benjamin, *Ursprung*, p. 287; Osborne, pp. 108–9.

8. Ibid., p. 288; Osborne, p. 109.

9. Cf. p. 12 of this book.

10. Cf. p. 39 of this book.

11. Hegel, *Vorlesungen über die Geschichte der Philosophie*, in *Jubiläums Ausgabe*, edited by Hermann Glockner (Stuttgart: Friedrich Frommanns Verlag, 1958), vol. 18, pp. 119–120; *Lectures on the History of Philosophy*, translated by E.S. Haldane (Lincoln: University of Nebraska Press, 1995), vol. 1, pp. 446–48.

12. Cf. pp. 17–18 of this book.

13. Benjamin, *Ursprung*, p. 288; Osborne, p. 109.

14. Ernst Bloch, *Das Prinzip Hoffnung* (Frankfurt am Main: Suhrkamp, 1959), pp. 1372 ff.; *The Principle of Hope*, translated by Neville Plaice et al. (Cambridge, Mass.: MIT Press, 1986), vol. 3, pp. 1167–71; cf. also *Der Geist der Utopie* (Berlin: Cassirer Verlag, 1923), pp. 279 ff.; *The Spirit of Utopia*, translated by Anthony A. Nassar (Stanford: Stanford University Press, 2000), pp. 218–25.

15. Benjamin, *Ursprung*, p. 284; Osborne, p. 105.

16. Aristotle, *Poetics*, translated by W. Hamilton Fyfe (Cambridge, Mass.: Harvard University Press, 1982), ch. 13, p. 47.

17. Ibid., ch. 14, p. 51.

18. Lessing, *Werke*, edited by J. Petersen (Berlin: Bongs Goldene Klassiker-Bibliothek, 1925), vol. 5, p. 172.

19. Schiller, *Kleinere prosaische Schriften* (Leipzig: Crusius, 1802), vol. 4, pp. 129–30.

20. *Schillers Demetrius*, edited by Gustav Kettner (Weimar: Verlag der Goethe-Gesellschaft, 1894), p. 210.

21. Julius Bahnsen, *Das Tragische als Weltgesetz und der Humor als ästhetische Gestalt des Metaphysischen* (Berlin: Van Bremen-Verlag, 1877). [Szondi does not provide a page number—trans.]

22. Eleutheropulos, *Das Schöne* (Berlin: C. A. Schwetschke and Son, 1905), pp. 147 ff.

23. J. H. v. Kirchmann, *Ästhetik auf realistischer Grundlage* (Berlin: L. Heimann, 1868), vol. 2, p. 29. Nicolai Hartmann writes in a similar vein: "The tragic in life is the demise of the high quality of human life." *Ästhetik* (Berlin: de Gruyter Verlag, 1953). [Szondi does not provide a page number—trans.]

24. Cf. my essay "Friedrich Schlegel und die romantische Ironie, mit einer Beilage über Tiecks Komödien," in *Schriften II* (Frankfurt am Main: Suhrkamp, 1978), pp. 11–31; "Friedrich Schlegel and Romantic Irony, with Some Remarks on Tieck's Comedies," in *On Textual Understanding and Other Essays*, translated by Harvey Mendelsohn (Minneapolis: University of Minnesota Press, 1986), pp. 57–74.

Chapter 13

1. *König Ödipus*, in *Sophokles: Tragödien*, translated by Emil Staiger (Zürich: Atlantis Verlag, 1944), vv. 145–46. "I'll do every thing. God will decide/ Whether we prosper or remain in sorrow." *Oedipus the King*, in *The Complete Greek Tragedies, Volume II: Sophocles*, edited by David Grene and Richard Lattimore (Chicago: University of Chicago Press, 1959), vv. 145–46, p. 17.

2. Schiller, in a letter to Goethe, October 2, 1797.

3. V. 1198 in Hölderlin's translation, *Große Stuttgarter Ausgabe*, vol. 5. "O, O, O, they will all come,/all come out clearly!" Grene, vv. 1183–84, p. 63.

4. Cf. Karl Kerényi, *Die Heroen der Griechen* (Zürich: Rhein Verlag, 1958), pp. 103 ff.; Albin Lesky, *Die tragische Dichtung der Hellenen* (Göttingen: Vandenhoeck and Ruprecht, 1956), pp. 63–64 and 193.

5. Cf. Emil Staiger, *Grundbegriffe der Poetik* (Zürich: Atlantis Verlag, 1946), pp. 196 ff.

6. Cf. Karl Reinhardt, *Sophokles*, 3rd edition (Frankfurt am Main: Klostermann, 1947), pp. 105 ff.

7. V. 357, in Hölderlin's translation; Grene: "You are the land's pollution," v. 353, p. 25.

8. V. 1179–80, in Staiger's translation; Grene: "saved the child for the most terrible troubles," vv. 1180–81, p. 63.

Chapter 14

1. *Das Leben ein Traum*, in *Calderon: Schauspiele*, translated by J. D. Gries

(Berlin: Nicolai Verlag, 1815), vol. 1, p. 199; "For those destined to melancholy, / their own merit is a knife-thrust, / since he whom knowledge ravages / is most apt to destroy himself!" *Life is a Dream: A Play by Pedro Calderón de la Barca*, translated by Edwin Honig (New York: Hill and Wang, 1970), p. 23.

2. [Spanish auto sacramental plays employ biblical, mythological, historical, or allegorical figures to comment upon Christian theology and, in particular, on the Eucharist. Seventy-three of Calderon's auto sacramental plays have survived, including a version of *Life is a Dream*—trans.]

3. Cf. Max Kommerell, *Beiträge zu einem deutschen Calderon* (Frankfurt am Main: Klostermann, 1946), vol. 1, pp. 218 ff.

4. *Das Leben ein Traum*, pp. 250–51; Honig: "for when a thing's impossible I find / the challenge to overcome it / irresistible; only today / I threw a man off the balcony / who said I couldn't do it. / So, just to find out if I can—what / could be simpler?—I'll let your virtue / go flying out the window" (p. 56).

5. Ibid., p. 251; Honig: "But what's a man like you to do / who is human in name only, / insolent, insensitive, / cruel, impulsive, savage, / and tyrannical, someone / born and bred among beasts?" (p. 57).

6. Ibid., p. 256; Honig: "Perhaps some day you'll see your own white hairs / become a carpet for my feet" (p. 60).

7. Ibid., p. 296–97; Honig: "What must be admits no remedy; / what's foreseen magnifies the peril, / impossible to cope with, / while to evade it only brings it on. / This is the circumstance, this is the law / grinding on so horribly. / The risk I tried to shun meets me head on; / and I have fallen in the trap / I took such pains to sidestep. / Thus I've destroyed my country and myself" (p. 88).

8. Ibid., p. 329; Honig: "So in endeavoring to free / my country of murder / and sedition, I succeeded / only in giving it away / to murders and traitors" (pp. 108–9).

Chapter 15

1. Paul Ernst, *Der Weg zur Form*, 3rd edition (Munich: G. Müller Verlag, 1928), p. 121.

2. *Othello*, act 5, scene 2, vv. 16–19.

3. Ibid., 5.3, vv. 360–62.

4. Cf. Hegel and Kierkegaard on Socrates.

5. *Othello*, 3.3, v. 357.

6. Ibid., 1.3, vv. 287–88.

Chapter 16

1. Cf. Walter Benjamin's differentiation between tragedy and mourning

play in *Origin of the German Mourning-Play*, which, however, also views *Leo Armenius* as a "martyr tragedy," that is, as a mourning play.

2. The spatial and temporal coincidence, respectively, of Leo Armenius's and Carolus Stuardus's murders with Christ's crucifixion could make the death of Leo Armenius (like that of the English king) look like a martyr's death. The differences between the two events, however, is so significant, especially in the dying men's attitude toward this coincidence, that Leo's movement toward martyrdom—as well as that of the empress Theodosia (see above, in text)—is to be understood more as a contrast between the tyrant and the martyr than as a direct interpretation of the tyrant as the martyr or their identification. A comparison of the two descriptions demonstrates this difference: "He felt that his strength had escaped him entirely,/As he gripped the wood on which the one hung,/Who dying, redeemed us, as he gripped the tree on which the world/Was freed of its fear, so that death may please/The one startled by hell. 'Remember that life,' he calls out,/'Which gave itself for your soul through this burden!/*Don't stain the blood of the Lord, which dyed this tree,/With the blood of sin! If I have carved out so many evil deeds,/Then out of fear of the one this tree bore/Take care not to strike Jesus' altar of reconciliation with a furious fist!*'" (*Leo Armenius*, vv. 2194–2203); "He demanded the deposit that the one who through His blood/Washed away man's guilt as the memorial of His suffering,/And the sign of precious favor left his wounded heart./Listen to the marvelous thing that happened here:/When Juxton opened the church book for his work,/The church book for which the prince had suffered so much,/For which England and Calidon disputed and denied him,/He found that the main story precisely for today/Was the one written by Matthew to the Christian people,/Where the Prince of Princes was injured by his own people,/Stood before His judge, and had to go pale on the cross,/Wounded by whip marks and sharp thorns./The king, who here almost remained deep in thought,/As if the bishop selected the story for his consolation,/Rejoiced in spirit and appeared truly born anew,/When Juxton placed the page in front of his face,/And showed him that this passage was usually read today./*The king took great pleasure that Jesus, through his suffering,/Recognized the same day as worthy of separating off and sharing with him./His spirit, having renewed its bond with God,/Appeared to be more refreshed and gladdened*" (*Carolus Stuardus*, Act 5, v. 100 ff., original emphasis). Both citations are from *Gryphius' Werke*, edited by Hermann Palm (Berlin: Spemann Verlag, 1883).

3. *Leo Armenius*, in *Gryphius' Werke*, vv. 524, 540, and 554.

4. Ibid., vv. 1643–46.

5. Ibid., v. 1784.

6. Ibid., vv. 1802–4.

7. Ibid., vv. 2417–16.

8. Ibid., vv. 2496–98.

9. Ibid., vv. 1129–31.

Chapter 17

1. The further observations in this first section follow Thierrey Maulnier, *Lecture de Phèdre* (Paris: Gallimard, 1943).

2. Vv. 634–40; *Phèdre*, translated by Margaret Rawlings (London: Penguin Books, 1989), p. 83. See also the lines that follow.

3. Vv. 284–88; Rawlings, pp. 51–53.
4. Vv. 685–89; Rawlings, p. 87.
5. V. 290; Rawlings, p. 53.
6. Vv. 196–200; Rawlings, p. 43.
7. V. 768; Rawlings, p. 95.
8. V. 1219; Rawlings, p. 133.
9. V. 1238; Rawlings, pp. 135–37. Cf. Maulnier, *Lecture de Phèdre*, p. 103.

Chapter 18

1. "*Warbeck*-Fragment," in *Sämtliche Werke, Säkular-Ausgage*, edited by Eduard von der Hellen (Stuttgart: Cotta Verlag, 1904), vol. 8, p. 143.

2. *Schillers Demetrius*, edited by Gustav Kettner (Weimar: Goethe-Gesellschaft, 1894), p. 109.

3. Ibid., p. 204.
4. Ibid., p. 94.
5. Ibid., p. 125.
6. Ibid., p. 28.
7. Ibid., p. 108.
8. Ibid., p. 226.
9. Ibid., p. 87.
10. Ibid., p. 219.
11. Cf. p. 77 of this book.
12. *Schillers Demetrius*, p. 100.
13. Ibid., p. 206.
14. Ibid., p. 155.
15. Ibid., p. 155.
16. Ibid., p. 107.
17. Ibid., p. 56.
18. Ibid., p. 99.
19. Ibid., p. 150.
20. Ibid., pp. 101–2.
21. Cf. the section on *Othello*, note 1.
22. *Schillers Demetrius*, p. 205.
23. Ibid., p. 167.
24. Ibid., p. 120.
25. Ibid., p. 205. Cf. my extensive presentation of this issue in "Der tragische Weg von Schillers *Demetrius*," in *Schriften II* (Frankfurt am Main: Suhrkamp, 1978), pp. 135–54.

Chapter 19

1. Heinrich v. Kleist, *Sämtliche Werke und Briefe*, edited by Helmut Sembdner (Munich: Hanser, 1952), vol. 1, p. 118 (act 4, scene 1).

2. Ibid., pp. 48–49 (1.1).
3. Ibid., p. 53 (1.1).
4. Ibid., p. 65 (1.2).
5. Ibid., p. 128 (4.4).
6. Ibid., p. 87 (2.3).
7. Ibid., p. 59 (1.1).

8. Ibid., p. 95 (3.1).
9. *H. v. Kleists Lebensspuren*, edited by Helmut Sembdner (Bremen: Schünemann, 1957), p. 42.
10. Kleist, *Sämtliche Werke*, vol. 1, p. 137 (5.1).
11. Ibid., p. 147 (5.1).

Chapter *20*

1. Georg Büchner, *Werke und Briefe*, edited by Fritz Bergemann (Wiesbaden: Insel Verlag, 1958), p. 27; *Georg Büchner: The Complete Plays*, edited by Micheal Patterson (Suffolk: Methuen, 1987), p. 26 (act I, scene 5).
2. Ibid., p. 50; Patterson, p. 49 (2.7).
3. Ibid., p. 80; Patterson, p. 78 (4.7).
4. Ibid., p. 56; Patterson, p. 55 (3.2).
5. Ibid., p. 374; Patterson, p. 290.
6. Ibid., p. 35; Patterson, p. 34 (2.1).
7. Ibid., pp. 69–70; Patterson, p. 68 (3.10).
8. Ibid., p. 27; Patterson, p. 27 (1.5).
9. Ibid., p. 42; Patterson, p. 42 (2.4).
10. Ibid., p. 29; Patterson, p. 28 (1.6).
11. Ibid., p. 45; Patterson, p. 44 (2.5).
12. Ibid., pp. 42–43; Patterson, p. 42 (2.4).
13. Ibid., p. 9; Patterson, p. 9 (1.1).
14. Ibid., p. 41; Patterson, p. 40 (2.3).
15. Ibid., p. 36; Patterson, p. 35 (2.1).
16. Ibid., p. 34; Patterson, p. 33 (2.1).
17. Ibid., p. 67; Patterson, p. 65 (3.7).
18. Ibid., p. 33 f.; Patterson, pp. 33–34 (2.1).
19. Cf. also Büchner's letter from March 1834. Ibid., p. 379; Patterson, p. 289.
20. *Danton's Death* thus anticipates the problem of the tragic death as it is posed for modern drama. Cf. Wilhelm Emrich's "Die Lulu-Tragödie" (esp. p. 223) and Beda Allemann's "Es steht geschrieben" (pp. 425–26), both in the second volume of *Das deutsche Drama*, edited by Benno von Weise (Düsseldorf: Bagel Verlag, 1960). Emrich's essay can also be found in *Protest und Verheißung: Studien zur klassischen und modernen Dichtung* (Frankfurt am Main: Athenäum Verlag, 1960).

MERIDIAN

Crossing Aesthetics

Maurice Blanchot, *The Book to Come*

Susannah Young-ah Gottlieb, *Regions of Sorrow: Anxiety and Messianism in Hannah Arendt and W. H. Auden*

Jacques Derrida, *Without Alibi*, edited by Peggy Kamuf

Cornelius Castoriadis, *On Plato's 'Statesman'*

Jacques Derrida, *Who's Afraid of Philosophy? Right to Philosophy 1*

Peter Szondi, *An Essay on the Tragic*

Peter Fenves, *Arresting Language: From Leibniz to Benjamin*

Jill Robbins, ed., *Is It Righteous to Be? Interviews with Emmanuel Levinas*

Louis Marin, *Of Representation*

Daniel Payot, *The Architect and the Philosopher*

J. Hillis Miller, *Speech Acts in Literature*

Maurice Blanchot, *Faux pas*

Jean-Luc Nancy, *Being Singular Plural*

Maurice Blanchot/Jacques Derrida, *The Instant of My Death/Demeure: Fiction and Testimony*

Niklas Luhmann, *Art as a Social System*

Emmanual Levinas, *God, Death, and Time*

Ernst Bloch, *The Spirit of Utopia*

Giorgio Agamben, *Potentialities: Collected Essays in Philosophy*

Ellen S. Burt, *Poetry's Appeal: French Nineteenth-Century Lyric and the Political Space*

Jacques Derrida, *Adieu to Emmanuel Levinas*

Werner Hamacher, *Premises: Essays on Philosophy and Literature from Kant to Celan*

Aris Fioretos, *The Gray Book*

Deborah Esch, *In the Event: Reading Journalism, Reading Theory*

Winfried Menninghaus, *In Praise of Nonsense: Kant and Bluebeard*

Giorgio Agamben, *The Man Without Content*

Giorgio Agamben, *The End of the Poem: Essays in Poetics*

Theodor W. Adorno, *Sound Figures*

Louis Marin, *Sublime Poussin*

Philippe Lacoue-Labarthe, *Poetry as Experience*

Ernst Bloch, *Literary Essays*

Jacques Derrida, *Resistances of Psychoanalysis*

Marc Froment-Meurice, *That Is to Say: Heidegger's Poetics*

Francis Ponge, *Soap*

Philippe Lacoue-Labarthe, *Typography: Mimesis, Philosophy, Politics*

Giorgio Agamben, *Homo Sacer: Sovereign Power and Bare Life*

Emmanuel Levinas, *Of God Who Comes to Mind*

Bernard Stiegler, *Technics and Time, 1: The Fault of Epimetheus*

Werner Hamacher, *pleroma—Reading in Hegel*

Serge Leclaire, *Psychoanalyzing: On the Order of the Unconscious and the Practice of the Letter*

Serge Leclaire, *A Child Is Being Killed: On Primary Narcissism and the Death Drive*

Sigmund Freud, *Writings on Art and Literature*

Cornelius Castoriadis, *World in Fragments: Writings on Politics, Society, Psychoanalysis, and the Imagination*

Thomas Keenan, *Fables of Responsibility: Aberrations and Predicaments in Ethics and Politics*

Emmanuel Levinas, *Proper Names*

Alexander García Düttmann, *At Odds with AIDS: Thinking and Talking About a Virus*

Maurice Blanchot, *Friendship*

Jean-Luc Nancy, *The Muses*

Massimo Cacciari, *Posthumous People: Vienna at the Turning Point*

David E. Wellbery, *The Specular Moment: Goethe's Early Lyric and the Beginnings of Romanticism*

Edmond Jabès, *The Little Book of Unsuspected Subversion*

Hans-Jost Frey, *Studies in Poetic Discourse: Mallarmé, Baudelaire, Rimbaud, Hölderlin*

Pierre Bourdieu, *The Rules of Art: Genesis and Structure of the Literary Field*

Nicolas Abraham, *Rhythms: On the Work, Translation, and Psychoanalysis*

Jacques Derrida, *On the Name*

David Wills, *Prosthesis*

Maurice Blanchot, *The Work of Fire*

Jacques Derrida, *Points . . . : Interviews, 1974–1994*

J. Hillis Miller, *Topographies*

Philippe Lacoue-Labarthe, *Musica Ficta (Figures of Wagner)*

Jacques Derrida, *Aporias*

Emmanuel Levinas, *Outside the Subject*

Jean-François Lyotard, *Lessons on the Analytic of the Sublime*

Peter Fenves, *"Chatter": Language and History in Kierkegaard*

Jean-Luc Nancy, *The Experience of Freedom*

Jean-Joseph Goux, *Oedipus, Philosopher*

Haun Saussy, *The Problem of a Chinese Aesthetic*

Jean-Luc Nancy, *The Birth to Presence*